WHEN THE ANGELS LAUGHED

EDDY SWIESON
tells his story
with Howard Norton

LOGOS INTERNATIONAL Plainfield, New Jersey

When the Angels Laughed
Copyright © 1977 by Logos International
All rights reserved
Printed in the United States of America
Library of Congress Catalog Card Number: 77-20584
International Standard Book Number: 0-88270-264-5
Logos International, Plainfield, New Jersey 07061

To Rini Tan,

my mother by adoption,

in gratitude for giving of

herself in love

Contents

Introduction—*Senator Mark O. Hatfield* vii

Foreword ix

1 The Beginning **1**

2 Growing Up **9**

3 War and Revolution **15**

4 Conversion **29**

5 Romance **45**

6 Faith **55**

7 The Harvest **67**

8 New Horizons **77**

9 The Voice without a Name **85**

10 The Challenge **93**

11 Adoption **103**

12 The Indonesians **111**

13 The Americans **115**

Afterword 121

INTRODUCTION

By Mark O. Hatfield

(U.S. Senator from the State of Oregon)

I am personally thankful to God for the living reminder that Eddy Swieson is of Christ's healing presence in our world. Eddy's story reminds me once again that the remorse of every biting recollection can be gathered up by the love and healing of Christ and transformed into gratitude over the joyful memory of His miraculous intervention in all our lives.

Certainly the words of the Apostle Paul ring true in this account of Eddy's pilgrimage: "For the sake of Christ, then, I am content with weaknesses, insults, hardships, persecutions, and calamities: for when I am weak, then I am strong."

The French writer-politician Andre Malraux has written that "one day it will be realized that men are distinguishable from one another as much by the forms their memories take as by their characters."

Eddy is known by those of us who love him, and now will be more widely distinguished, for the way his memory of the intervention of God in his life proves to him that in his weakness Christ's strength has been made perfect.

I have been reminded once again that what counts in this world is the life of Christ within us breaking through the alienation and pain and restoring us to the Father and to one another. For, as I marvel along with Eddy over his miraculous recovery from near-death, from blindness, and crippling illness, to his present healthy life and productive ministry, I marvel as well over the love of God and Christ revealed to all of us in other miraculous ways.

Washington, D.C.
November, 1977

FOREWORD

The angels must have had a good laugh when they learned who it was that God had chosen to be the future associate pastor of the 150-year-old Fourth Presbyterian Church in Washington, D.C.

It sounds, even now, like a divine practical joke.

For the Lord had put His hand, in 1932, on a tiny Chinese-Indonesian baby, not even a normal healthy baby, but one who was, at the age of three weeks, dying of malnutrition on the floor of a shabby hut in the slum area of a Chinese ghetto near Surabaya, on the island of Java.

Moreover, it was a baby born into Buddhism, and to a family with a long tradition of ancestor-worship. And when this story began the baby's poverty-stricken family was waiting only for the child to breathe its last, to complete preparations for its burial.

Now, forty-five years later, nobody is laughing. It is clear, now, to all who have heard the story, that God, as usual, knew what He was doing. In making His choice, He did it the "hard way" as a dramatic demonstration of the intricate and mysterious manner in which the seemingly disconnected events in the lives of all of us can be dovetailed together to accomplish His divine purpose.

For this demonstration the Lord chose the life of Eddy Ie Swieson, the "dying baby" whom He snatched from the gates of death in the Java slum and saved from blindness and crippling illness, and then from death when the Japanese seized his home village, and from murder by fanatical rebels.

This book tells the story of the transformation of that dying Buddhist infant into one of America's most distinguished and fruitful servants of Jesus Christ. It is the life story of the man known now to many thousands as Dr. Eddy Ie Swieson, L.Th., D.Min., Bible scholar, linguist, eloquent preacher, and the author of a continuing course of Bible study that is being used in a growing number of churches of many denominations from coast to coast.

To the large and growing congregation of Washington's enthusiastically evangelical Fourth Presbyterian Church, he is simply "Eddy," their beloved associate pastor.

Howard Norton
November, 1977

WHEN THE ANGELS LAUGHED

chapter 1
The Beginning

When Eddy Swieson was born into the poverty-stricken Chinese family of IkDjoen Ie in a slum area of Java, near Surabaya, the world had fallen on hard times. Peoples and governments everywhere seemed to have lost faith in the future because of dismal failure in the past. Depression was spreading fast. There was not enough work, not enough money, not enough food, not enough medicine; in short, times were bad and getting worse. So, that year, the future was less than promising, even for healthy babies. The year was 1932, the lowest year of the Great Depression.

But nobody anywhere in that era of suffering could have had less hope than Eddy Swieson, whimpering and dying alone on the floor of a darkened room in one of the shabby shacks of a Chinese ghetto.

His parents, themselves undernourished and without money or the skills necessary to earn money, could see no way to keep their newest baby alive, so they had decided it would be the kindest thing just to let him die. Their four other children already were suffering the ills of malnutrition. They could not all be saved.

So they wrapped little Eddy in rags and laid him on the floor of a room adjoining the area where the family gathered. And they closed the door because they couldn't bear to listen to his slowly weakening cries. But at that point there was a knock on the front door. It was Rini Tan, and although she was Eddy's aunt, she was not aware at that moment of Eddy's existence. Rini was childless, because of some physical complication, and she had an overflowing supply of love for children.

What happened next is best told by Rini Tan herself:

I went into the family room and made small talk for a while with my brother and sister-in-law, Eddy's parents. But I began to notice that every time the conversation stopped for a moment, and there was silence in the room, I seemed to hear a strange, faint, whimpering sound, like a kitten that wants to get back in out of the yard.

This happened again and again, and it seemed to me that the sound was coming from an adjoining room. Finally, I got so curious that I just got up and walked over to the door of the room where the sound seemed to come from. And when I opened it, all I could see in the semi-darkness was a little bundle of rags on the floor. I moved closer, and I thought I saw a slight movement from inside the bundle. And then I heard again that faint whimpering sound. It came from inside the bundle.

I knelt on the floor and pulled aside the rag, half-expecting to find a kitten inside. But, I was surprised—yes, shocked—to find instead a newborn baby! Nobody had told me that there was a new member of the family. And it was obvious, even there in the dark, that this baby was very, very sick. He was nothing but skin and bones. His tiny stomach was bloated from starvation, but even then it wasn't any bigger than a tennis ball. He looked so fragile and so sick I was, at first, afraid to touch him. So I rose and hurried back into the family room.

"Where did this baby come from?" I asked, though the

question sounded foolish before I got it out. "Nobody told me that you had another child! Why didn't you tell me? Are you going to just sit there and let this little child die? Don't you know he is almost dead now? Have you called a doctor in? Why aren't you doing something? This is callous and cruel! You must not let him die!"

Anger and fear for the baby rose within me, and I scolded the parents in words that I would not like to repeat. But they just sat there and shook their heads helplessly, while I continued my tirade. And finally, when I gave them a chance to speak, they confessed to me, reluctantly and with a show of shame, that there was no money for a doctor; in fact, no money for food or anything else, so they had decided it was best for them to try to save the older children, and let this weak baby die.

Well, that cooled my temper tantrum, and I spoke to them in kinder tones.

"Why didn't you tell me?" I asked. "Here," I said, handing them some money from my purse, "is some money for food. Now you go and get something for the others to eat—and you look like you are starving yourselves. And while you are doing that, I am going to take this baby to a doctor."

I didn't even wait for a word of permission. I just strode back into that darkened bedroom and knelt, again, beside the pile of rags. The baby, Eddy, I saw, again, was so fragile that I just didn't dare to pick him up. I was afraid I might break one of his tiny bones. So I went to the bed and borrowed a small pillow, and I put the pillow down on the floor beside the baby and literally scooped Eddy from the floor and sort of rolled him onto the pillow without actually lifting him from the floor. And with Eddy and the pillow in my arms, I rushed off to the hospital in our little suburban town of Modjokerto.

I guess I didn't really expect to get much help, even from the hospital because Eddy was pretty far gone, and our grubby little

3

hospital was not the kind of a place where you would expect to find a reputable doctor. But, then, I didn't realize at the time—I was then a practicing Buddhist—that the Lord Jesus Christ was using me to accomplish His purpose, which was to save Eddy for service to the body of Christ.

Well, I rushed through the door of the hospital and looked hurriedly about the outer office for someone who could help me. There was no one in sight. But as I turned around a young Dutchman came through the door from one of the wards. And since he was wearing a stethoscope around his neck, I took it for granted that he was a doctor, and before he could open his mouth I was pouring out the whole story about how I had found this starving baby on the floor and that I was afraid the baby was dying, and would he please do something, quick!

The doctor nodded, and without a word, he took the pillow and the baby in his arms and went into a nearby office. It was only then that I noticed he was wearing a small name plate, which announced that he was Dr. Weese.

I looked him over rather sharply, because it seemed to me that he was awfully young to be a real doctor—too young, maybe, to be a *good* doctor, anyway. And while he examined Eddy, I plied him with questions:

"Are you a real doctor?" I asked. And after I had asked it I realized that it was rather an insulting question. And since I wanted this man—doctor or not—to help save Eddy I hurried on with another question to try to cover up the first. "Where did you go to school?" I asked quickly.

Little by little, as he examined Eddy from head to toe, his story came out. Dr. Weese was just out of medical school. And he had just come out from Holland to serve his internship at this terrible, rundown hospital. And then the miraculous news! His specialty, he said, was pediatrics; he was a doctor who specialized in taking care of children. And this baby, my own little Eddy, was his very first patient as a practicing pediatrician.

Well, I couldn't decide whether to be nervous over the fact that he was such a new doctor, or to be happy over the fact that taking care of babies was the work he was trained to do. So I decided that I could be both nervous and happy at the same time. And his very next words gave me my first bit of hope that Eddy might, after all, have a chance to live.

"This baby is my first patient," he said, "and I cannot, I will not, start my medical career by losing my first patient. So I promise you," he said, turning and looking straight into my eyes, "that this baby is not going to die! This baby is going to live!"

That made me feel a little better, but I stayed right there in the hospital with Eddy most of that first day and far into the night. I wanted to make sure that this young man was, indeed, what he said he was. It turned out that he was even more than he claimed to be. He was not only a doctor, but a man of infinite compassion. That first night he was right beside his tiny patient almost until dawn. And when I returned to the hospital early the next day his eyes were heavy from lack of sleep. So I told him that I would watch the baby for a while, and urged him to take a nap, which he finally, reluctantly, did.

For over three months—for one hundred days, to be exact—that's the way it went. Dr. Weese grappled with death, and tiny Eddy clung precariously onto life. Gradually, toward the end of February, 1933, the improvement in Eddy became so marked that even in my moments of deepest pessimism I could not deny that the doctor was winning his first big battle.

And then came that happy day when the doctor greeted me with a victorious smile as I entered the hospital for my morning visit.

"I think he's strong enough, now," he said. "You may take him home, if you will promise to do what I tell you, and not make him sick again by giving him foods that are too rich, or spoil him and make him a crybaby by too much attention." The doctor flashed a boyish grin after that remark. It was obvious to me, at that moment, that the doctor loved Eddy, too, as much as I did. And that it was not only his pride in the success he had with his first patient that brought tears to his eyes when I wrapped Eddy in a blanket and started toward the door. He was going to miss this tiny life that he had saved.

I turned to wave a final goodbye as we reached the hospital door, but Dr. Weese already had turned his back and was rubbing one of his eyes with the corner of a handkerchief and complaining about "the dust" that was always blowing into the interior of the hospital when the doors were opened. I looked around, but there was no cloud of dust that I could see.

Now three months had passed since I found Eddy dying on the floor of my brother's rundown home. In those three months, Eddy had become my own child, and my love for him could not have been any greater if he had been born to me.

I knew he was going to need constant care, but it never seemed like a burden to me. I honestly thought of it as a privilege. I knew I could never have a child of my own flesh. But Eddy, the child of my brother and sister-in-law, was, in a very real sense, a child of my own flesh—my father was his grandfather, just as it would have been had Eddy been born of a union of my husband and myself. I felt strongly that Eddy was mine because I had helped to save his life; because there would not be any Eddy if I had not snatched him away from his natural parents. So I vowed solemnly that I would never allow anyone to take Eddy away from me. And I determined, in my heart, to make this adoption legal, if that were possible, even if it took my whole life to do it. I had no idea, at the time, how nearly accurate was my estimate of the length of time it would take to achieve my goal of legal adoption.

Not long afterward, the young doctor came to my home for a visit, and to check up on Eddy's health. As we sat in the parlor I could see that he had a problem on his mind, so I made small talk and waited for him to say what he had in mind to say. And finally he did get to the point.

"My wife and children," he said, "are going to return to Holland soon. And I have been giving this a lot of thought. I know how much you love Eddy. But I wonder if you love him enough to give him up, for the sake of his own future. I wonder if you love him enough to let me send him to Europe with my family. He can get a good European education there, and make something of himself. I have a deep conviction that this little boy has talents that he should be given a chance to develop. I am sure you have sensed that I have a very deep affection for him and that I would gladly adopt him and bring him up as my own son.

"Please sleep on this. Don't decide right now. Think it over. There is time. I think you will decide that in Europe he would have a better chance in life. And I'm sure you would have many chances to see him as he grows to manhood."

I knew in my heart that this moment would come, but still I was not prepared for it. Many times I had told myself that if the doctor or anyone else ever asked me to give up Eddy I would turn them down flat. But now, I found myself wavering. The very thought of giving up "my son" tore my heart, but I knew the doctor was right, that Eddy's chances in life would improve with European training. So, after a few moments of silence I heard myself tell the doctor that I would indeed think it over. And we shook hands, and he departed.

That night, and for many other nights, I wrestled with the problem. What could I offer him? Only a mother's love. I went to the temple and prayed before my ancestors and asked their advice. I sat through many hours of Buddhist meditation. But it

7

was not until almost the eve of the departure of the doctor's family that I came to a decision.

"Dr. Weese," I said, "you are a kind and compassionate man. I am forever in your debt. But I think that Eddy needs a mother's love more than anything else. And I think, too, that I need Eddy as much as he needs me; You have done wonderful work, and I will pray that the great Buddha will reward you richly, but I have decided to keep Eddy here with me."

So the doctor's family left for Europe. Months later we heard a report that the ship on which they traveled had never reached Holland, and had probably run into a severe storm and capsized, with the loss of all on board.

Although the report was never confirmed (the doctor himself had moved to another city), I went again to the temple to thank the great Buddha and burn incense on his altar, because he had put it in my heart to keep Eddy with me in Java.

It was years later, after I became a Christian, that I came to realize that Buddha had nothing to do with that decision, that it was Jesus Christ who had planted that love in my heart and that it was the Lord who led me to make the right decision, even though I was the follower of a pagan religion at that time. The Lord does, indeed, work in mysterious ways.

chapter 2

Growing Up

At this point, Eddy takes up the story.

I did my best to be a normal, mischievous boy for the first eight years of my life, despite the fact I always seemed to be just getting over, or just coming down with one or another of a wide assortment of illnesses. From what my mother told me about my shaky start in life, I thought I was lucky to be alive, even though physically weak. And any boyish fun I could manage was a welcome bonus along with the gift of life itself.

My foster mother was a no-nonsense disciplinarian, the kind that the Bible applauds. And in spite of my constantly frail state of health I knew that I was risking some stinging corporal punishment every time I violated the parental precepts.

One of the best-enforced rules of my childhood was that I must *never* under any circumstances smoke anything: cigarettes, cigars, pipe, dried grass, tobacco, corn silk or anything else.

Now any eight-year-old boy will tell you that any parental order that is so strict and absolute presents a challenge that no eight-year-old boy can resist. That was the way it looked to me, anyway.

The big chance for some illicit smoking came to my eight-year-old social set every time there was a wedding. And there were a lot of weddings, because the Chinese residents of Java tended to have big families. We would dress up in our best like good little boys and move around obediently among the wedding guests. And, taking care that nobody was watching, we would snatch a cigarette or a cigar and stuff it into a pocket. To us, it didn't matter that the illicit bit of tobacco might already have been half smoked and discarded, although we did prefer the unused cigarettes and cigars to the secondhand ones.

When we had grabbed enough of them to give everyone a few puffs, we would disappear, one at a time, and reassemble in the woodshed or some other outbuilding that was out of sight from the main house, and there we would experiment with the smoking materials we had filched.

I was always a ringleader of these secret experiments with worldly pleasure. And despite the precarious state of my health, I smoked right along with the healthiest of them until my head began to spin and my breath smelled like the inside of a chimney that needed sweeping.

Inevitably, my mother charged me with the crime, and every time I opened my mouth to lie about it I breathed a distinct air of guilt in her face. My mother, without speaking a word of disapproval always went to the corner of the kitchen where she kept a piece of stout rattan and gave me a lesson in the wages of the sin of disobedience.

There were other kinds of illicit fun interspersed with spells of illness during this quiet, but physically painful time of my life. There was, for example, the "banana parade" game. It was easy to play, and we all thought it uproariously funny.

We would sit on a roadside bench and watch the grown-up girls promenade up and down the street in the evening in their fancy clothes. And, as the evening shadows began to fall, the game was to eat the bananas we had brought along and then carefully toss the skins along the sides of the street where the girls were walking in their wooden-soled slippers. As past masters of the sport we knew exactly what would happen when one of those wooden soles stepped on a banana skin. The result was instantaneous and dramatic. It never failed.

Thinking back over the years, I don't think my mother ever found out what we were doing out there in the early evenings, and I'm quite sure I was never punished for it. I hope the young ladies who were our embarrassed victims have found it in their hearts by now to forgive us.

The end of this period of boyish fun and games came about 1940, just before the Japanese entered World War II. Despite my mother's best efforts I became more and more anemic and my health began to decline alarmingly.

Now Rini Tan, my foster mother, had taken some training as a nurse, and she knew a bit about the basics of modern medicine and the science of nutrition. And she developed some ingenious substitutes for the remedies we were unable to purchase on the open market.

To strengthen the bones in my spindly legs and arms, for example, she went into the mountains with shovel and bucket to find some natural lime. She dug out a supply of it—as much as she could carry—and brought it home. There she put it into a large earthen jar, filled with water until all the lime had settled to the bottom and a large part of it had been dissolved in the water. Dipping the clear limewater from the top of the jar she forced me to drink it, day after day and month after month. And to my surprise it worked. There's nothing weak and spindly now about my arms and legs.

But I was weak, and I needed vitamin B, which wasn't available anywhere in Java at the time. And again my mother proved equal to the challenge. She searched for, and finally found, a supply of rice husks which, she said, contain some of the most effective nutrients in the rice plant. She ground the husks into a powder, added some sugar and water and other things I cannot recall, and when the mixture was completed she pronounced it vitamin B. Now whether this mixture had any of the properties of vitamin B I'm not in a position to say, but I do know that it worked just as effectively on my weakened body as the limewater had worked on my brittle bones. I began to regain my strength again, and my hope of getting strong enough to go back to school began to rise. I had missed years of school because of my precarious state of health, and I can honestly say that I wanted to go to school. I loved to study and I really enjoyed my time as a student.

But just as I began to think I was strong enough to go back to the classroom I was laid low again by a new sickness. I contracted malaria.

It was all but impossible to get quinine to ease the attacks of malarial fever, so my mother turned to the artificial quinine, called Atabrine, a remedy well-known to American veterans of the war in the South Pacific. It was a bitter-tasting pill, and after constant dosage it turned the skin of a malaria sufferer from its natural tone to a sickly yellowish.

Along with the attacks of malaria came spells of pleurisy, pneumonia and stomach disorders. My stomach, in fact, suffered continually from the crude substitute medicines that I was taking. Even though they did prove effective in the end, they were pretty hard to take, and there were a number of unfortunate side effects. The limewater, for example, was extremely bitter and it invariably made me sick for an hour or so, at least, every time I drank it—which was almost every day.

Malarial attacks came about every month, and every attack left me weaker. And as I grew weaker I fell ill more frequently with the maladies that accompanied the malaria.

The most alarming thing that ever happened to me started

about this time. My eyesight began to fade, probably as the result of the mixture of medicines I had been taking. And for a period of two years I was almost completely blind, and that, of course, blasted my hope of returning to school. But in spite of my sickness and my extremely weak condition, my mind remained alert and active and I continued to long to get back to my studies.

My mother fought desperately to bring me back to health, especially after I began to go blind. A devout Buddhist at the time, she tried everything the Buddhist priests suggested to her, and she frequently called in for consultation the local "dukun," a kind of Javanese witch doctor supposed by the Buddhists to have the power to chase out the evil spirits that caused various kinds of illness. The method she used—our "dukun" was a woman—was to get the evil spirits out of the house where they would not have such a close-range shot at me. So she would go into a sort of dance through the house and around it on the outside—a dance of exorcism—and she would chew up a mouthful of foul-smelling herbs and spit them out all over the place as she danced. Then she would collect her fee and depart.

But the spirits that were guests in our home must have found it too comfortable to give up, for the witch doctor's efforts didn't seem to do me any good. But we followed her directions to the letter. She had advised us to hold a full-moon festival—a "selamatan"—every month to keep the spirit happy. It was a very expensive brand of preventive medicine, because the festivals were elaborate, but we took no chances. They were held every month while I was ill, and even afterward, just in case of a relapse.

One awful day, I remember, I fell from a moving vehicle as it bounced across some railroad tracks, and they tell me I was unconscious for several hours. When I finally opened my eyes the first thing I saw was this ugly "dukun" dancing around me and spitting all over me from her mouthful of stinking herbs.

My worried mother was standing by wringing her hands and crying. As I opened my eyes and asked what had happened, the "dukun" gave a whoop of victory, broke off the spitting and collected her fee. She was gone almost before I could scramble to my feet.

I was now years behind classmates of my own age, but my health did finally begin to improve. The malarial attacks came less often, and finally the great day came, and I returned to the classroom, eager to catch up with those who had been fortunate enough to stay in school while I was sick.

I studied night and day, and was moving up fast when I was blocked by an unexpected development from another source: the Japanese, who struck Pearl Harbor on December 7, 1941, swept southward through the Philippines and attacked the island of Java where we lived.

My foster father, who for years had operated a moderately prosperous trucking business, was put out of business when the Japanese seized his trucks. And the financing of the family fell to my mother who was the proprietor of a small factory making handmade native Javanese fabrics.

Attendance at school became spotty after the initial attack by the Japanese. Whether we attended or stayed home depended on the location of the day's fighting. So, from the time of the initial Japanese attack until quiet was restored by the Japanese occupying forces, attending school became only a sometime thing. Fortunately for my education, the Japanese made quick work of the task of overwhelming the Dutch forces that were defending the island at the time of the 1942 assault. But, for a ten-year-old boy, the war was the most excitement he had ever witnessed in his brief span of life. And, secretly, I hoped the fighting would go on for a long time. The thought of danger never entered my mind.

chapter 3

War and Revolution

The top of a cherry tree looked like a great place to sit and watch the war. I was ten years old, and I loved the action. It didn't occur to me that there was any real danger, or that people were being killed, and that my own family at any time might be next on the list of fatalities.

There were a few minor irritations. I still remember my father's livid outrage when the Japanese forces seized his trucks and left him without any way to support the family. And even my mother, who was normally a kindly, even-tempered woman, used expressions I did not realize were in her vocabulary when Japanese soldiers ransacked our house and took our supply of food.

But we were not seriously inconvenienced by either of these acts of war. My parents were canny enough to foresee some such action, so we had hidden resources the Japanese never found, and we never suffered any real hunger.

Schools were closed during the initial assault early in 1942, and that was a blessing to me, because I had decided that I wanted to be a general and command a lot of troops and I was determined to learn how it was done by watching the generals in action from the top of our cherry tree.

And what a show it was, for the short time it lasted! Fighter planes streaked overhead, diving toward targets that were just out of sight from my perch in the cherry tree. I would watch them flash by, then listen closely for the rattle of machine gun fire and the dull thud of exploding bombs. It was just like the movies, only it was real, it was really happening. What could be more fun?

Then, one day, as I climbed down from my perch, the war got too close to be fun. I was just about to go into the house when I heard gunfire close by. This was too good to miss, I thought, and I turned and started back toward the cherry tree. But my mother, pale with fright, rushed from the house, grabbed me by the arms, and pulled me back inside and pushed me flat on the floor.

Suddenly, we could hear bullets striking the wall. We hugged the floor, trying to make ourselves as flat as the mats that covered it. And we waited and waited for what seemed to be hours, motionless and quiet. At last, my mother rose, and I got up, too. And only then did we see how close death had come. Along one wall of the room where we had taken refuge there was a neat line of bullet holes, about three feet above the floor level. Standing, we would have been hit, possibly killed. Once again, God had provided a miraculous escape. And once again Buddha got the credit, along with our ancestors. My mother dutifully went to the temple and thanked both Buddha and the spirits.

Then came chilling news. My grandfather—my mother's father—was seized by the Japanese MPs. He was taken to a concentration camp, tied to a tree and beaten, and, later, starved to the point of collapse. He told us that they ridiculed him and kicked him around between beatings.

His house was confiscated, and converted into an emergency

station where the wounded were brought. The trees, every day, were decorated with hanging human bodies, hoisted high to ease the stench. Two or three times a week the soldiers would cut them down, stack them like firewood, douse them with gasoline and burn them. That was the only funeral they got.

We heard from the grapevine that the jails were not too bad. Not crowded at all, our informants said, because the Japanese were using an efficient method of weeding out the excess prisoners. They were shooting them. But there was evidence, also, of great cruelty. We saw many bodies unspeakably mutilated.

One day the soldiers rounded up all the local residents they could find and herded them into a park. They had caught ten alleged thieves, and when we arrived on the scene under escort, the thieves had been tied to separate poles and stripped of their clothes. After the soldiers were satisfied with the size of the audience ten MPs stepped forward, with pistols loaded, and each stood before a separate victim and pumped three bullets into the bodies.

These moments were frightening, but we were fortunate. The shooting did discourage the stealing, but the news passed from neighbor to neighbor told of scores of atrocities. Women were attacked and then murdered. Property was stolen, householders tortured in their own homes, and then tied to their own furniture and cremated when the house was put to the torch.

But aside from my grandfather's painful experience, no one in the family was seriously hurt.

Food was scarce and we were using corn and tapioca as substitutes for the rice that was our usual diet. We had to take good care of our clothes because there was no clothing to buy. There were no medicines for the sick. And, as usual, I was sick; not just once, but often.

17

When the Japanese finally surrendered, in 1945, we rejoiced that peace had returned, but it had not. Immediately, there was a fierce and bloody revolution against Dutch rule of the islands, led by the late Mr. Sukarno. And this was many times worse than the Japanese invasion—at least for the Chinese—because the revolutionaries suspected the Chinese of being pro-Dutch, and it was a time of torture and death for many of our friends. It was an anti-Chinese pogrom.

Every morning human bodies floated down the river past our house, most of them with bamboo sticks piercing their chests or stomachs, and many with heads missing, or with hands and feet chopped off by torturers.

Our trucks were seized again, by the revolutionaries, and my worried father grew ill-tempered and battled frequently with my mother. After every major domestic battle my mother would grab her belongings and take me by the arm and go to my grandparents' house to stay for as long as two months.

It was during one of our sudden visits to my grandparents that we had one of our closest escapes. Every day someone we knew was being killed, so we stayed indoors as much as possible. Early one evening, while my cousin and I were studying in our room, there was a crashing sound as two terrorist gunmen broke down our front door and rushed into the house with guns cocked and pointed at us. They rounded up the whole family and took us into the living room while they started a search of the premises.

Grandpa, who was half-blind, was trembling with outrage. To the horror of all the rest of us, he decided to frighten them out of the house by shouting at them, and threatening to have each one of the terrorists executed by a firing squad—though we couldn't imagine how he expected that this would scare them, since he had no firing squad under his command. He had only his family.

We were frozen with fright. We were sure he would anger them and they would shoot us. But grandpa kept on yelling. And to our amazement the pair of ruffians went out the door hurriedly and took to their heels.

But as soon as they left, we ran to the back porch to rebuild our courage, and we ran smack into another pair of gunmen who were beating our servants. This second pair apparently had been sent to the rear to guard the house and prevent our escape. But when they saw us running free, and their own colleagues in the midst of a running retreat, they grabbed their guns and fled, too.

Well, grandpa was the family hero that day. "All you have to do is scare them," he said in a tone of authority. "You see how easily they frighten."

We were pretty well shook up, but my grandfather was equal to every occasion. He assembled us in the dining room and gave us a lecture on self-defense. "Next time, you cowards," he said, "do something to scare them. Don't leave it all to me. Here's what we will do. Get a lot of broken drinking glasses and all the other broken glass things you can find, and put them on top of every tall cabinet in the house and tie strings to the piles atop each cabinet. If these outlaws come again, just pull the strings and make all those glasses crash to the floor at the same time. That will get rid of them."

We looked at each other, but nobody seemed to be able to think up any plan that seemed more promising, so we dutifully gathered broken glassware and set the traps.

Every night for several days, before we went to bed, we took turns checking our booby-traps. Finally, in broad daylight, at a time when we least expected them, there was another terrorist attack on our house. A glance out the window made it clear that they had us surrounded. All of them had guns, pistols, even tommy guns.

19

Two of them came in and jumped on my grandfather's secretary in the office, and broke open the safe. They took what they wanted, and left. And not until after they were all gone did any of us remember that we had not pulled the glassware down from the cabinets to frighten them. Grandpa was furious.

One morning, a short time later, I was working on my bicycle in front of the house, when I heard something that sounded like a bunch of firecrackers being set off. I stood up on the bench where I had been working, and could see a group of marines, probably half a dozen, surrounding the house directly across the street.

They began to fire at the house, and there were answering shots from inside the house. I dropped to the ground, quickly, and crawled to a nearby bush to watch the battle, just yards away. I was frozen with fear that they would come next to our house. Now and then there was a human scream from inside. Later we learned they had trapped a guerrilla group in the house and wiped them out.

As my military expertise grew, from watching these skirmishes, I took mental note that having a squad of marines scout quietly on foot was a much more efficient and successful way to eliminate the enemy than to call a truckload of soldiers accompanied by tanks and other noisy equipment, as was frequently done. The noise of the tanks and the trucks always tipped off the guerrillas that they were being stalked, so they usually got away. The marines, I thought, were clever to use silence and surprise. When I become an officer, I thought, I will remember this lesson.

The guerrilla tactics were to sneak into a private home, and open fire on the Dutch troops who patrolled the streets. It was tough on the families who lived in, and were forced to say in, those houses during the battle. Many died.

Often, when a Dutch trooper entered a private home during

the day, when the guerrillas were in hiding, they would make that home a target the same night. They were known to gun down all the women and children in the house and then torture the head of the house to death. This was to discourage local residents from cooperating with the beleaguered Dutch regime.

Sometimes terrorists, disguised as sellers of fruits and vegetables or rice, would pass along the street and visit each house, and before leaving they would slip a note secretly to the householder demanding that he place a gallon of gasoline in a convenient spot, to be picked up by the guerrillas the same night. The gasoline was to be used to manufacture Molotov cocktails.

When we were given such notes, there was nothing to do but comply. To refuse was death. On the other hand, if the Dutch marines had caught us providing gasoline to the rebels, the punishment also was severe. It was a time of genuine terror. And we did not wonder when we saw daily truckloads of human bodies being hauled away to be burned. We knew, pretty well, why they had been killed. And we wept for them.

There was also constant danger of guerrilla looting of private homes, and it was the Chinese—because the Chinese controlled the island's economy—who were victims of the worst of the looting. Often the looting was followed by burning of the home, and those families who were allowed to leave the houses before they were set fire considered themselves lucky.

The home of my grandparents on my father's side was one of the many that were destroyed by fire.

Because of the looting and the burning, it was common practice for a family to bury its jewelry and other valuables in the ground, leaving no marker to give away the hiding place. The result of this was that when the revolution ended, after four long years, many families had great difficulty finding their valuables, having forgotten the exact spot where they were buried.

21

The Sukarno revolution did finally end, but to us who were very young it seemed endless. There had been seven years of constant war between the outbreak of fighting in World War II in 1942 and the end of the revolution in 1949.

We had become hardened to the sight of bodies drenched with blood. And after spending hours hiding under beds and other pieces of furniture we were never surprised when we found the streets outside our home littered with the bodies of humans and animals, waiting to be carted away.

Looking back now, as an adult, and realizing the terrible dangers that surrounded us and trapped us during both the war and the revolution, I realize that it was only through God's infinite mercy that we did not lose a single member of our family through all of those nightmarish seven years.

For the Japanese, Indonesia was the richest prize of World War II. They had to seize it quickly, because it was the closest major source of oil. And without oil, their whole war machine would collapse. So they rushed southward while Pearl Harbor was still burning and made quick work of wiping out the tiny Dutch force that was supposed to defend the islands. And the Japanese Navy was pumping oil from the fast-flowing wells of Borneo while the assault on Java and Sumatra was still under way. Oil that flowed from some of the wells was so free of pollutants that it could be used to fire ships' boilers without refining.

It was Indonesia that kept the Japanese factories supplied also with tin, copper, rubber, lumber, bauxite and nickel for the three years that the Japanese military ruled the islands. Strangely, there was scarcely any sign of resentment among the native Indonesians over this snatching of their natural resources by an invading enemy. But the Japanese had studied history and they had sent scouts among the islands of Indonesia for years before the war, and they saw a unique opportunity to grab the wealth of the Indonesian islands while at the same time winning the friendship and support of the Indonesian natives and their leaders. Here's the story of how they did it.

For almost a hundred years before the outbreak of World War II, there had been a continuous and rising flow of immigrants from China to Indonesia. They came from the overcrowded provinces of Kwangtung, Fukien and Kwangsi Chuang. They came at first in search of jobs on the newly formed plantations in the middle of the nineteenth century, dazzled by the promise of a better life on these rich islands. Then the Dutch rulers discovered the mineral wealth of the islands and the Chinese came to get the high pay (by Chinese standards) that the new mine owners were giving to attract miners. By the early years of the twentieth century, the Chinese were coming by the hundreds of thousands; there were so many, in fact, that the Dutch government of the islands slammed the door against all further immigration from China. But in a country made up of more than three thousand islands, how could the door be closed? The Chinese population kept on increasing. There simply were not enough border guards to watch the hundreds of thousands of miles of shoreline. The "wetback" Chinese rowed or swam ashore at night from the hundreds of colorful junks that sailed silently among the islands, ostensibly as trading ships. And it was not until the Great Depression of the 1930s eliminated the demand for labor that the flow of Chinese immigrants slowed and then stopped. Some of the immigrants returned to China, but the eighty or ninety years of Chinese immigration gave Indonesia a permanent population of more than two million Chinese, hundreds of thousands of them already Indonesian citizens by birth, and since the Chinese tend to have big families, their numbers on the islands continued to grow until today there are an estimated four million Chinese there, most of them born on the islands.

Now the Chinese, since ancient times, like the Jews and the Indians, have an inherited talent for business. So when the job market evaporated in the Indonesian islands they turned to their inherited talents. Barred by colonial law from buying or owning farm land, they became shopkeepers, then money lenders, bankers, wholesale merchants, exporters, importers, shippers, factory owners, technicians, and artisans. And before the 150 million Indonesians realized what was happening, the four million Chinese in their midst had gained a firm control of the whole Indonesian economy.

It seems to be human nature to resent an inflow of foreigners, and especially when those foreigners are as clannish as the Chinese, and even more so when those foreigners are so successful that they take the local economy away from the natives who lived there before the foreigners arrived.

By the time of the outbreak of World War II resentment of the Chinese domination of Indonesia's economy was running high among the natives. So when the Japanese loosed their blitz and snatched the wealth of Indonesia away from the owners, it was the Dutch and the four million Chinese who suffered most, not the 150 million native Indonesians, most of whom were farmers and workers.

That began decades of discrimination and suspicion against the Chinese in Indonesia.

Native political leaders, including Sukarno and Suharto, two of the future leaders of the country, willingly cooperated with the Japanese invaders. It was the Chinese and the Dutch who came under suspicion and were searched and harassed by the Japanese, because they were the ones who had lost the most in the invasion, and seemed the most likely to retaliate.

Then, three days after the Japanese surrendered, on August 17, 1945, the pro-communist Sukarno launched his revolution, and the whole round of property seizure and harassment of the

Chinese and Dutch began all over again, and lasted another four years, until 1949, when Indonesia won its independence from Holland.

The arrival of peace, at last, in 1949, brought even more troubles to the Indonesian Chinese. The destruction of the Indonesian economy caused by the war was made worse by the peace. The victorious Sukarno clamped a dictatorial "guided democracy" on the Indonesian state. A strict system of foreign exchange controls virtually trapped the Indonesian population on their individual islands. It eliminated almost all chance for foreign travel.

Import and export controls killed off much of Indonesia's booming foreign trade, and built up a mountainous trade deficit, and an even more mountainous national debt. Control of shipping restricted movement even between the islands, some of which were under rebel factions and in a state of war. There was censorship of the mails, the telegraph and telephone systems, and Sukarno's spies were everywhere.

Evangelistic work and missionary work among the islands was almost at a standstill because of the paralysis of internal life under the communist-tinted "guided democracy" of Sukarno.

Indonesia had been a glittering temptation to exploiters, conquerors and colonialists throughout history. When Christopher Columbus accidentally discovered America in 1492, he was disappointed because it blocked what he had hoped was a shorter route to Indonesia. Even in Columbus' day, Indonesia had been enjoying a high level of civilization for more than a thousand years. The people now known as Indonesians are the product of intermarriage of several different groups of Asians who ruled the islands over the centuries.

The Buddhist kingdom of Srivijaya, from the seventh to the

twelfth century, ruled the islands now known as Indonesia and much of the rest of southeastern Asia from a capital established on Sumatra.

In the fourteenth century the Hindu kingdom of Majapahit dominated the same geographical region from a capital in Eastern Java. These two early kingdoms have given the Indonesians a legacy of temples and other ancient structures that rank among the world's finest examples of ancient art. They also had an important influence on the physical and other characteristics of what we now call the native Indonesians.

Islam started to infiltrate the islands in the twelfth century, and it has now replaced Hinduism in all the islands except Bali. Today, ninety percent of the Indonesians are professing Moslems, five percent are Christians—about half of them Roman Catholics—and the rest a scattering of Hindus, Confucianists and others.

The Portuguese arrived in the sixteenth century and established trading posts. By this time the once-powerful Indonesian kingdoms had been broken up into small states which were unable to stand up against Western colonial incursions.

The Dutch began arriving in 1602 and quickly took over colonial rule of all the Indonesian islands, and kept the control for most of the next three hundred years.

The British snatched control away from the Dutch briefly, during the Napoleonic period in Europe, but with the fall of Napoleon the Dutch resumed control and developed Indonesia—with the help of a few million hard-working Chinese—into one of the world's richest colonial possessions.

Agitation for independence got under way in Indonesia about the start of the twentieth century, led by a small group of young professional men and students, most of them educated in the Netherlands. A number of the leaders of the country, including

Sukarno, were imprisoned by the Dutch for long periods for their political activity.

For ten years after Indonesia got its independence in 1949 the country was politically fragmented among a large number of small parties, and there was a long succession of short-lived national governments. In 1957 there was a succession of rebellions in Sumatra, Sulawesi and other islands which so discredited the parliamentary system that Sukarno met little opposition when, by his own personal decree, he set himself up as a strong independent executive in 1959, and aligned the country's foreign policy with the Asian communist states.

Only the Indonesian Army remained outside Sukarno's absolute control. By 1965 evidence of mismanagement and misconduct by the Sukarno regime became overwhelming. And when the Indonesian communist party then attempted to prevent the loss of its power by murdering six top generals of the army, General Suharto was able to defeat the coup by force of arms and forced Sukarno to hand over to him political and military power, in 1966. Sukarno remained for a time as a figurehead president, but was voted out of office by the People's Consultative Assembly in 1967, and went into retirement until his death in 1970.

General Suharto, elected to a full five-year term as president in 1968, won the respect and admiration of the country for his moderation, and was re-elected in 1973.

Under Suharto, Indonesia has turned its back on ideological extremes and set as its top priority goals the economic rehabilitation of the country and improvement of the living standards of the people. The domestic and international economic and financial ruins left by the Japanese and by Sukarno and his communist-backed regime probably will not be wiped out entirely for decades.

27

chapter 1

Conversion

There's a special kind of fear that goes with Buddhism. I was haunted by it as a boy of seventeen, about to graduate from high school. It wasn't death that I was afraid of so much as life; specifically, the life that I believed would come after death. After seventeen years of almost continuous illness I was, at last, beginning to feel pretty good. And I wanted to get through to some kind of higher power and convince Him that I deserved some years of enjoyment before having to take my chances on the next life. I was full of self-pity, and I was afraid the Almighty, whoever He was, might not have heard what a hard life I had just been through, and He might order me reincarnated as one of the lower animals in the next life. For I firmly believed in the Buddhist "wheel of life" doctrine—that we all have to be reincarnated numberless times, and in many different forms of life. I had nightmares about coming back to life as a stray dog or a cricket.

Well, it was about this time that a Dutch friend gave me a copy of the New Testament in the Dutch language. Dutch and Indonesian were my only languages then. I thanked him, profusely, like a true Oriental, and put it in my pocket. When I got home I took it out of my pocket and put it up on the top shelf with some of my last year's school books. I didn't even open it. That shelf was my discard pile.

I used to lie in bed and look out the window at the big, tropical Indonesian moon, and wonder what the future had in store for me. The more I wondered, the more I worried. And the more I worried the more depressed I got, until I wept into my pillow without really knowing why.

As the only son of my foster parents I knew what was expected of me. It was my duty to take over, eventually, the business my father had chosen. My dad operated a small trucking business, and my mother, a woman of energy and independence, had a business of her own, a small factory manufacturing Indonesian "batik" fabrics. But I was a frail youngster and the very thought of having to boss a crew of burly, brawling truck drivers scared me and gave me bad dreams. Thoughts of taking over the batik factory didn't scare me, they only bored me. "What an awful life that would be," I told myself. But what to do? It was my duty. One or the other. And I hated both options. So I turned over and wept some more.

One morning when I was brooding and getting nowhere it struck me that it might help to lock my door and go into a long period of Buddhist meditation. So I turned the key, loosened my shirt at the collar and took up the prescribed stance, cross-legged on the floor.

"Now, how do I start meditating?" I thought. I bowed my head and shut my eyes, but nothing came. So I sat up straight and stiff and tilted my head upward and closed my eyes again. Still no powerful thoughts, just a mental blank. I was facing the wall that contained my bookshelves, and every time I opened my eyes with my head tilted upward, the first thing I saw was that little black Dutch New Testament.

"But, no," I told myself. "This is no time for reading. This is a time for thinking. I must plan my life. I must think of Buddha, or, at least, think of some way to spend my life that does not involve trucks or batik fabrics."

So I closed my eyes again and again. And every time I opened them there, again, was that little black book that I had never opened. So after a while I got to thinking about the books on that shelf. From my position of meditation on the floor I looked at them, one at a time. I had read them all, I thought, and as I looked at each book I tried to recall what was in it. This, I told myself, is a good way to start meditating. I'll just start thinking about those books. They are all good school books, and I will get some good thoughts. At least, I'll be thinking about something, not just sitting here helplessly with a blank mind.

So I started down the bookshelves, book by book. I always liked to study, and I soon found that I could give a pretty good synopsis of what was in every one of them. This went on for hours, I thought. Probably it was only a short time. But, anyway, I finally reached that top shelf. And only halfway across it, reciting the content of each volume as I came to it, I finally reached the little black book that I had accepted as a gift only a few days before, and had never opened.

"What shall I do?" I asked myself. "This is a time for important meditation. My whole life may be changed by the thoughts I have today. So I'd better stick to my meditation and my thoughts. If I start reading now, I'll lose my train of thought," I argued. But then it occurred to me that I really hadn't developed any train of thought. I was just reciting the lessons contained in a lot of old school books, and I knew every one of them by heart. The only one I couldn't review in my mind was that little black book. So I might as well read it, or at least look at a few pages. Then maybe I could honestly say that I had read every book on all of the shelves and was able still to give a good

31

account of what was in them.

"It's such a small book," I noted mentally, "there can't be very much in it."

So I unfolded my stiffened legs and arose painfully from the floor, rubbing the circulation back into the legs as I straightened them, and stretching my arms above my head to take the kinks out of my back. Then I climbed onto a chair and plucked the little gift volume from the top shelf and settled down again on the floor, my back propped against the bed, and opened it.

As if ordered by some mysterious power, the New Testament opened at the beginning of Paul's letter to the Christians at Rome. I began to read, with no real interest at first, and thought to myself that this Christian holy book seems awfully dull. But I read on. And finally I came to the passage in which Paul describes God's anger at the evil ways of people who prevent the truth from becoming known, and His anger at those who worship idols, and at the people who insist on worshiping the things that God had created, instead of worshiping the God who created them! This passage set my heart pounding faster. It was an idea, a conception of the relative importance of things that had never occurred to me. I began to feel twinges of conviction and guilt.

"This is exactly what I have been doing," I said aloud. "This is what we have all believed all of our lives! Can we be wrong? I must read on and see what more this man has to say. Maybe this is the Almighty one speaking to me. Maybe my fears and my decision to meditate were all arranged by Him to lead me to this book. Anyway, these are certainly new thoughts to meditate. Now I am getting thoughts that may be worthwhile. I'll read some more. I can meditate later. Why had I never had such thoughts? Why did it never enter my mind that the wonders of nature are not so great, could never be so great as the wonders of the God who created it all?"

It was an exciting new picture, to me, of the relationship of man to God. And I could hardly wait to turn the little pages to find out what would come next. I read on where Paul describes the thought of these evil people as "nonsense" and pictures their minds as filled with emptiness and darkness.

"This book makes some sense!" I thought. My own mind, I recalled, had been filled with emptiness and darkness for several hours just passed. I had not had a new or constructive thought, I had only recited things that I had read and memorized in books. And not a single one of those books had been so excitingly new and mind-expanding as this one.

"But to accept this Jesus as my Lord and Savior? No way! He seems to have had some good ideas. But to give up my ancient Buddhist faith for this new foreign guru? No, sir. It's going to take more than a few new ideas, even if they do seem to be very interesting and important.

"But I will read more." So I settled down against my bed, with my legs stretched out on the floor and went on with the reading.

Then, suddenly, it was as if I had been struck by a bolt of lightning! I came to the fifth chapter of Romans and what, to me, was an incredible revelation: "Now that we have been put right with God through faith, we have *peace with God* through our Lord Jesus Christ," I read, and my heart began to pound even harder, with the excitement of the words. "He has brought us by faith into this experience of God's grace, in which we live. For when we were helpless, Christ died for the wicked, at a time that God chose."

"Peace with God!" I almost shouted. "That must be it! That is the answer. If I have peace with God I don't have to be afraid of the future, or of the next life, or of anything else."

Behind my excitement—which may not be understandable to the Western mind long familiar with the teachings of Christ—was an Oriental conception of peace that is a lot like the idea the Jews express with the word "shalom." It denotes more than simply the cessation of war. It implies a complete peace, through the whole man—peace spiritually, physically, socially and mentally. It implies the experience of God's infinite grace in this life, and then on through eternity.

I threw my head back and leaned on the bed for a moment and thought of the wonder of such a peace with God, the supreme being of the universe. And suddenly I felt an overwhelming compulsion to speak directly to this new God, to ask for mercy in the name of Jesus Christ, His Son, who, according to this wonderful little book had come to earth to save all people, and had wiped out our sins by the sacrifice of His own life!

And then I heard myself say it aloud!

"Lord Jesus Christ, forgive me," I said. "I didn't know! I didn't know! I have been blind and ignorant. Forgive me!"

And there was suddenly a feeling within me like an explosion. It was a surge of unutterable joy!

Then I became conscious of another presence in the room! I felt as if hands had been placed on my head and shoulders. I turned and looked quickly around, fully expecting to see this new guru, this Jesus, right there in the room with me. No other presence was visible, but I knew deep within me that Jesus must have been there, for my feeling of extreme elation continued and grew.

Finally, I could not restrain myself another second! I jumped to my feet half-laughing, half-sobbing, and rushed out the door into the back yard as if the house was on fire behind me.

Overcome completely by my intense feeling of ecstasy, I ran through the yard embracing each tree, kissing each plant, and each flower, laughing and shouting as if I were drunk with joy, which I guess I was. But my feeling was one of overwhelming joy and adoration of God, the God who had opened such wonders to me in the Bible, His book. How clearly it was written! Nowhere in Buddhism or animism, with its thousands of gods—one behind every bush, so to speak—had I ever found any such direct and distinct statements, so clearly put, about the relationship of the maker of the universe and the creatures that He had created.

If St. Francis of Assisi had been there in my back yard and seen me, he would have understood perfectly; he would immediately have known that I was praising the Lord by this effusive greeting of nature, and I know that he would have been pleased, because he understood this kind of thing. But I have often wondered, since, what my Buddhist friends would have thought had any of them happened to drop by at that moment. They probably would have tackled me and thrown me to the ground and then called for the men in the white jackets to come and get me.

But for me it was a day of wonder!

I suddenly felt that everything in the world was new. And even my outlook was new. The world had in a flash become a place of boundless wonder instead of the pit of torment that I had pictured in my depression and brooding early in the day. I felt an extreme delight to be a part of it all—and I felt that it was all mine. I felt so much joy that I began to weep. And when the thought of my friends, and millions of other humans, not yet released from the fears and sorrows and worries of their man-made religions, I wept again. "I must tell them," I said aloud, "I must tell them.

"What awful mistakes we have been making," I thought. "And we have no excuse. For, as the Apostle Paul wrote: '. . . What can be known about God is plain to them, because God has shown it to them. Ever since the creation of the world His invisible nature, His eternal power and deity have been easy to perceive in the things that have been made. So they are without excuse. For although they knew God they did not honor Him as God, or give thanks to Him, but became futile in their thinking, and their senseless minds were darkened. . . . [They] exchanged the glory of the immortal God for images resembling mortal man or birds or animals.' "

That passage hit me right between the eyes. For, as animists, we had been worshiping old trees, birds, stones, reptiles, just about anything and everything, in fact, that God had created. But we had never turned our worship toward God, our creator.

On returning to the darkness of my room as the evening fell, I sat in the dark and pondered this enormous thing that had happened to me. The truth of Paul's letter to the Romans cut me like a knife and left a throbbing sense of guilt. I had found the truth. I knew as a Buddhist that Gautama Buddha had never attempted to answer the mystery of death and what comes after it. But Jesus offered assurance of life beyond this world—a life of happiness and fulfillment, not a return trip to this world in the form of some lower animal. Jesus offered assurance of life beyond the present life because He conquered physical death. My Buddhist teachers had told me that I would have to wait through a long cycle of deaths and reincarnations before I would find eternal peace. But Paul had brushed aside this "nonsense" showing that Christ had eliminated the need for punishment; by dying on the cross He had removed our sins. Peace with God was available to us immediately. "What a wonderful truth to know!" I thought. "I must tell everyone."

Looking back now, over the twenty-eight years that have passed since that day, I can see that the most important lesson in that whole glorious experience was the fact that I, a staunch pagan for seventeen years, was converted to Christianity by simply reading the New Testament alone in my locked room, with no teacher, preacher or missionary to instruct me! I read it, the truth was clear, the words of the Apostle Paul convicted me of my error and my sins, I asked to be forgiven, I accepted Christ by faith as my Savior and I was transformed from a brooding pagan into a joyful member of the body of Christ—all before I had ever spoken to another Christian. The Bible did its own missionary work.

I had a strange dream that changed the whole direction of my life only a few weeks after I had given my life to Christ.

One hot summer afternoon I lay on my bed with my Bible beside my pillow and I must have dropped off to sleep. At least I think I went to sleep. What I experienced was so real that I still am not sure whether I was sleeping and dreaming, or whether I saw a vision. Suddenly I saw a man come into the room. He was partly bald, and he was wearing a semi-saffron robe, somewhat like the robes the Buddhist monks wear.

He was looking straight at me, and he seemed to be pointing at something, some kind of a book. I sat up quickly to get a closer look at the man and at the book he was pointing to, and to ask what he wanted in my room, but the sudden movement must have awakened me, if I was, indeed, sleeping, and when I looked around the vision had vanished. There was no one else in the room.

But it was all so vivid, so real that it left me trembling with excitement. I thought about the significance of that dream for a long time, and decided there was no doubt the book was the Bible. I asked myself "Was it the Lord who caused this vision or dream?" The more I thought about it, the more convinced I became that it must have been a sign that God wanted me to devote my life to that book. This was the beginning of my long road from paganism to the Christian ministry. When my father, some time later, angrily protested my decision to attend a Christian college and study for the ministry, that vivid dream helped me stick to my decision. And every time I wavered in my resolve, when the burden of studies became heavy, the dream came back to haunt me, and to remind me of what I believed to be a sign from God that He wanted me to go to work for Him.

From the very day of my conversion I have been a constant reader of the Bible.

In my first year as a Christian—my freshman year, so to speak—the New Testament was my whole Bible. I had only a vague knowledge that the Old Testament existed. But I devoured that little New Testament. In that first year alone I read it through one hundred times, until I had long portions of it committed to memory. I awakened every morning when the roosters began to crow, about four, and I would sit or lie there in bed and saturate myself with the Holy Scripture.

In these early months I was baffled by the unmerited love that God had bestowed on me. I wept a lot as I read. And it puzzled me why such a large part of the human race was so callous and ungrateful for this divine love.

My father, who was still a Buddhist and Confucianist, worked himself up into a fury every time he caught me reading my Testament. I was actually afraid he might have a heart attack in one of these tirades, so I tried not to irritate him. He threatened to disown me, to throw me out of the house, and to thrash me. But I already was sufficiently schooled in the teachings of Jesus to know that a soft answer was called for. And I knew that in his heart he loved me, and that he had no intention of carrying out his threats.

I guess I became a fanatical Christian in my first year. A little education is a dangerous thing. And I had had only a little Christian education, and that came entirely from reading the New Testament, with no one to interpret or explain. More important, I had never read a word of the Old Testament.

So I was worried that my human weaknesses seemed to stay

with me. I wanted to emerge from my conversion a full-blown saint.

I punished myself cruelly for my shortcomings in that first year. Probably this was a hangover from my years of Buddhist and Hindu teaching. I carved a crude crucifix for myself and knelt before it every night. And I kept a written record of my failures and shortcomings—my sins—even of every rebellious thought that entered my mind. As punishment for these things I would force myself to take my bitter Atabrine tablets without the help of a glass of water or iced tea. I was still required to take these tablets to ward off attacks of malaria.

But I soon realized I was making the Christian life unpleasant. When I was a Buddhist I had been taught that suffering was a sign of devout faith. But there was nothing in the New Testament that said I had to force sufferings on myself to prove that I was a Christian. Then, about a year after my conversion, I first got hold of a copy of the full Bible, including the Old Testament. And that provided the missing link I needed to bring my new-found Christianity into its true perspective.

For months I devoured the Old Testament as eagerly as I had the New Testament in my "freshman" year. And it finally dawned on me that the great men of the Bible were not themselves perfect, after all. They all fell short of perfection many times. This lifted a great burden from me. And, so far as I can recall, I never afterward forced myself to take a bitter pill without iced tea to blot out the taste. It was the Old Testament that freed me to be patient, with a clear conscience, while I waited for the Lord to mold me into the kind of man He wanted me to be.

I read the story of Jeremiah, a man who ministered to kings in the name of the Lord. And I marveled that even this holy man weakened to the point where he not only complained to God, but got so upset he even cursed his mother and father for

39

bringing him into the world, and called on the Lord to destroy just about everyone who had come into his life!

If Jeremiah could get away with that, I reasoned, then the Lord wasn't going to be too angry over my rebellious thoughts. God made it clear in the Book of Genesis that humans are, after all, half dust and half deity, and the dusty half is bound to come through on occasion.

I admire the wisdom we can find in the Psalms, despite the psalmist's frequent use of poetic license.

One of my favorites in those early days was the picture drawn in Psalm 1 of the godly man who grows like a tree beside a stream of water, a tree that bears fruit in its season, and is not expected to bear fruit all the time, though its leaves remain green.

I took comfort, also, in Paul's exhortation to be patient because our Christian growth only starts at the moment we accept Christ. He says in the second letter to the Corinthians that if we get in step with the Lord we will eventually be transformed, by the presence and action of the Holy Spirit, into the likeness of Jesus Christ himself.

In my early Christian days I literally slept with my Bible. I underlined every new passage as I found it. In fact, I underlined so many that it eventually became easier to find those that were not underlined. And the most important thing I learned was to be patient. There is no such thing as an "instant Christian."

One of the most significant events of my early Christian life occurred in the late 1940s. I still regard it as definite proof that God is still working the old-time biblical miracles among us today. This is what happened:

My grandmother, on my mother's side, became seriously ill. Now at that time, as I recall, only my mother and I had accepted Christ. My grandfather was so bitterly anti-Christian that he vowed to burn every Bible that came into his house. It made him furious that my mother and I had "surrendered" to this "Jesus propaganda." At the same time, he was an equally strong believer in Buddhism; he might have been described as a Buddhist zealot or radical. My grandmother was less radical, but solidly Buddhist.

Shortly after she became ill, the family was summoned to her bedside. She had lapsed into a coma and it looked as if we were going to lose her. My grandfather, a well-known architect, was prostrate with grief. The two were very close and extremely affectionate to the end of their days.

Grandmother was in a coma for three days, unable to eat or drink. And in those days intravenous feeding was unknown, so three days without food or water meant she was surely about to die.

Mother and I prayed that the Lord would spare this gentle old lady. She was the mother who had shaped the character of my own beloved foster mother, and it seemed to me that if the Lord let her die I would not be able to stand the suffering it would cause my own beloved mother.

But the rest of the family took a more practical view. They went out and bought a coffin, and contacted an undertaker to make plans for the funeral.

As my grandmother sank near death, one of my uncles, a son of my grandmother and grandfather, suggested, somewhat fearfully, that if we wanted to call a Christian pastor to pray it would be all right "if grandpa would permit it."

To our amazement, grandpa, in his grief, agreed. The doctors had declared her a hopeless case, so he undoubtedly felt this was no time for a squabble in the family.

So the local pastor was called. When he arrived at the bedside, he was greeted politely by grandpa and was told that he might "say whatever prayers you Christians say." The pastor, kneeling beside the bed, raised his face toward heaven and quietly asked the Lord, "if it be thy will," to save this beloved lady and give her more years of life to enjoy with the family she has worked so hard to bring up.

After his prayer, we sat in silence around the bed for a time. And then we began to notice, for the first time in days, a movement of the eyelids and the hands. We all thought this must be the end, and we drew close. As we did, my grandmother opened her eyes wide and began to struggle to sit up. Several of us reached out to help her, and she looked about with a curious raising of her eyebrows and asked us to bring her a glass of milk and some porridge. She said she felt especially that a glass of milk would taste good and might do her some good.

With puzzlement written all over our faces, the family quickly complied with her request, and we stood around watching as she drank the milk. Then she turned to the members of the family and asked, "Which one of you invited that delightful stranger to come and visit me here?"

We looked at each other, not knowing what to say, thinking that poor "dying" grandma was a little out of her head. But she kept on asking about the stranger. And when we insisted that none of us had seen any stranger, she proceeded to tell us that we must have been blind and she told this story:

"This gentleman was dressed in white," she said. "He wore a shiny robe, and his face was so pleasant, and it seemed to radiate light like the sun, and he had the most beautiful long hair.

"He came right over here to my bed and told me, 'Please drink a glass of milk and eat something and you will be well.' And as he turned to go, he told me, 'Don't be afraid.'

"That's why I asked for a glass of milk, and now that I've had it, I must say I do feel much better."

From that moment on, grandma rapidly regained her strength. But the most radical change was in grandpa. He was firmly convinced that the Christian pastor had done the healing by calling on the Christian God to perform a miracle. He dropped his Buddhist faith on the spot, and became one of the most active Christians in the region. And grandma, too, and most of the other non-Christian members of the family came to Christ with him.

And as the news of the miracle spread through the city, many who knew my grandfather and his bitter anti-Christian bias, were convinced that Christ was the true Savior and gave their hearts to Him. The story of my grandmother's healing is still being told in the churches there.

And, speaking of churches, my architect grandfather immediately went to the pastor who had prayed for grandma and arranged for the construction of a new church building. Constructed late in the 1940s, that building still stands, and it is still filled to overflowing with believers every Sunday. The faith of many of them dates back to grandmother's illness.

Before he died, grandfather had designed and built a half dozen churches in Eastern Java, three of them in the capital city, Surabaya.

The miracle of my grandmother's escape from death convinces me that real old-time Bible miracles are being used by the Lord to help bring the pagans to Christ. The time is late, and I am sure that nothing short of miracles will bring them to abandon their ancient man-made religions. I often wonder if the same kind of miracles may be happening all around us here in this sophisticated American society, and we, perhaps, are too sophisticated to accept them.

chapter 5
Romance

I was hopelessly in love. And I was in torment.

To me, it really did seem hopeless. She was a smiling, friendly dark-eyed girl with long, shiny black hair and a voice that sounded to me like the tinkling of silver bells. When she sang, I knew she must be an angel in disguise. And when she looked at me, I got chills and stammered. I was certain she would not want to marry a skinny, spindle legged Chinese like me. And I had good reason for my fears. Deborah—that was her name, but everyone called her Debbie—was Chinese, too. But there was an invisible wall between us. She was a different kind of Chinese. It was sort of like the Hatfields and the McCoys, only there wasn't any shooting.

In Indonesia, even now, the Chinese community is sharply divided. There are the so-called "overseas-Chinese"—those who have lived abroad for generations and adopted the traditions and customs of their adopted land; and then there are the "Chinese-Chinese"—the families that have migrated from China in recent years, and who still cling to their own Chinese dialect (there are many) and the customs and traditions of old China.

45

The two groups have always avoided social contacts. They speak to each other only on business matters. Usually they have difficulty understanding each other because the overseas Chinese, especially those in Indonesia, abandoned the Chinese language generations ago. What was even worse, in my lovesick eyes, was the snobbery that grew up between the two groups. Do you see my impossible problem?

I was an overseas-Chinese, I spoke Dutch and Indonesian and I had always been taught to look down on the Chinese-Chinese as social and intellectual inferiors.

Debbie was a Chinese-Chinese, she spoke beautiful Mandarin Chinese, and a sufficient amount of Indonesian when necessary, and she had been brought up by strict parents who warned her against having anything to do with those vulgar, mongrel, money-mad overseas-Chinese, who couldn't even speak their own language. Naturally, I assumed she was a dutiful daughter and would obey her parents.

We were both students at a Christian college on the island of Java, and my first ray of hope came when I learned that Debbie's father was a devout Buddhist-Confucianist, and that she had defied him and accepted Christ as her Savior. And even more significant, in my frantic, scheming mind, was the fact that she had stood up to her pagan father again in choosing a college. He gave in finally, and allowed her to attend this Christian school.

I could sympathize was the plight of Debbie's father, I thought. How could any father be angry at this lovely girl, or refuse her anything she wanted? I worshiped her. And all my hopes hinged on the vital fact that she was a Christian and I was a Christian and that, I hoped, would reduce the height of that impassable wall between us. Maybe.

So I continued to worship from a distance for a time, doing my best to concoct plots that would make it necessary for me to speak to her. I had not counted on the intervention of a miracle to bring us together, but there was to be a miracle just ahead and if I had known it, I would have been saved much lovesick misery.

The miracle came about like this. Our school was Chinese-oriented, and much of the class work was in the Chinese language, some in English and some in Indonesian. So when the school authorities found that I, an overseas-Chinese, had absolutely no knowledge of any Chinese dialect they decided that I should have a Chinese language tutor, and take an intensive course in the language so I could keep up with my studies.

That was when the miracle happened!

There was a knock on my door the afternoon after I had been told that they would send me a tutor. I opened it, and there stood Debbie—my own lovely Debbie—smiling shyly at me and holding a Chinese-language Bible under her arm! It was Debbie the school authorities had picked to teach me Mandarin Chinese! I was so overcome that I didn't even hear what she said to me, at first. And when I didn't reply, she repeated, again, that she had been sent to teach me Chinese. And still we stood in the doorway. Finally, I regained my senses and invited her to come in, but I still could not believe what was happening. It must be a dream! And it certainly was a miracle, an answer to my secret prayers!

Debbie was very prim and businesslike. She announced that she had brought the Chinese Bible along because she had been told that I was familiar with the Bible in the Dutch and Indonesian languages. So it had occurred to her that the Bible in Chinese would be the very best kind of a textbook for me.

I agreed eagerly. But, of course, I would have agreed with anything she said at that moment, so anxious was I not to disrupt this wonderful thing that had happened. And we started that very afternoon with the first of my lessons in Mandarin Chinese.

It had never occurred to me that Debbie Giam—Giam was the family name—might be very intelligent, as well as the most beautiful and desirable girl in all of Indonesia, if not the whole world. I remember that first day I sat there in a sort of trance. Every time she looked down to read from her Chinese Bible, I would stare at her, drinking in every detail, from her beautiful hair to her dainty feet. And then when she looked up I would quickly shift my gaze back to the Bible in my own lap, and then fail completely to follow her in the proper Mandarin pronunciation. I could see that my lovely teacher was not too happy with my progress that first day, and that frightened me. I banished the thought that she might give up in disgust and ask the school people to send someone else in her place. So I resolved to try to get control of my emotions the next time, and show her that, even though I was one of the overseas-Chinese that her class looked down upon, I wasn't dumb.

So now, wonder of wonders, I had a legitimate excuse to be with Debbie for a time every day! And I did the best I could to make skinny Eddy Swieson look and act like a man she might consider as a husband.

Part of my plan was to study the Mandarin Chinese language as I had never studied anything before, and in this way, perhaps, impress her that I was smart, if not the handsomest man on the campus. So that's the way I studied, early and late, and I always waited eagerly for her arrival the next day.

I began to notice that my teacher had begun to relax, and was less shy and we engaged more frequently in small talk about things apart from Mandarin Chinese. I also began to notice that I was learning a lot about the Chinese language. And Debbie was quite frank in her comments to me. She said she was very happy with the way I was learning. And I, of course, was profuse in my praise of her talents as a teacher.

After three months of this, I was able to read many passages from the Chinese Bible quite well. And Debbie had completely abandoned her shyness, and she would actually clap her hands in applause when I finished a particularly difficult passage with minimum errors. I noted this secretly in my heart, and told myself, "You're making good progress, Eddy." I did *not* mean progress in my studies.

After six months I found that I was understanding most of the lectures of the Chinese professors, even the most intellectual of them.

After only nine months of study with Debbie there came a wonderful day when the dean of students asked Debbie how I was doing, and on the basis of her report the dean asked me to serve as an interpreter from Chinese into Indonesian for some of the Chinese instructors! I remember that day particularly, not because of the honor of being asked to interpret, but because I used the excitement of the moment, and took advantage of the obvious look of pleasure in the eyes of the beautiful Debbie, to do something I had never dared do before. I took her in my arms and held her close for a moment, my cheek against hers, and whispered my thanks into her ear. She pulled away quickly and gave me an embarrassed smile. But my heart leaped with joy! "I think she likes me!" I said to myself. So I quickly told her that we must continue with the lessons.

"I want to learn Mandarin Chinese well enough to preach a sermon in it," I told her. "You must continue to help me." She smiled in a way that I thought was a happy smile, and said she would continue, and then she added, "The school said I should teach you for one year, and we have been studying together for only nine months." And again I felt a pang of fear. Was she doing this because the school asked her to or because I did? I would have to intensify my campaign of conquest. I vowed silently to myself that when I preached my first sermon in

49

Mandarin Chinese, Debbie Giam would be sitting in the congregation to share my accomplishment as my proud bride-to-be, and not simply as the teacher who made the sermon in Chinese possible.

And that's the way it happened. Those last three months of study with Debbie strayed away from strictly Bible study and wandered off frequently into conversational Chinese and into some very personal subjects, like the beauty of her complexion, the shine of her hair. And then we began to talk of our plans—our individual plans—for the future. I found that we both had a call to spread the gospel. I told her that a wonderful singing voice like hers would be a tremendous help in Christian crusades. In that way, our plans for the future began to grow together. Until finally, we knew that God had meant us for each other, and the formal words of proposal seemed superfluous when I finally summoned up the nerve to say them out loud to Debbie, as I had practiced them hundreds of times myself before a mirror.

We were gloriously happy together for about one day. Then we faced the sobering fact that her Buddhist father, who literally hated the Christian religion, and my newly Christian parents, who still clung to the ancient Chinese tradition that it's the parents who do the matchmaking, had never been told what was going on.

How to break it to them?

My mother, like a lot of other mothers who have only one son, was always jealous of my girl friends, and was inclined to be sharply critical of them, too. She was always furious when I switched girl friends without first consulting her. And she never failed to disagree with my choice. Although I loved her dearly, I was still a little afraid of her. She had always been such a stern disciplinarian. But I felt that she was seldom right in her criticism of my feminine friends.

I remember the one she said she disliked most of all. It was the girl I was keeping company with when I first caught sight of Debbie, and I had told my mother that I was thinking seriously of asking her to be my wife. Well, my mother let go with such a tirade against this girl that it shocked me. She was really a fine girl and a beautiful one, and came from a good family. And now, many years later, my mother knows she was wrong in that instance, because the young lady I parted company with in favor of Debbie is now a Christian missionary in West Irian, the Indonesian half of the island of New Guinea.

Debbie had already overruled her father in the matter of her choice of the Christian religion and her choice of a Christian college. So we felt it could be done again, in the matter of a husband.

But my mother, frankly, had us scared. We didn't want to launch our married life with a family battle. So we spent hours planning how we would break the news to my foster mother, Rini Tan, and to my father. They were both staunch members of the Hatfield-McCoy feud with the Chinese-Chinese faction. They were disdainful of these relatively new arrivals in Indonesia (Debbie's father migrated from Fukien Province when he was fourteen years old. But that looked like a short time ago to my parents, who were both born to families that had lived in the Indonesian islands for generations.)

Even while we worried about the plan for breaking the news of our love for each other, the Lord stepped in with another miracle to help our romance along. It didn't look much like a miracle at first, because it started when I got sick. There was a persistent pain in my stomach that would not go away. It got so bad, finally, that my mother and father rushed over to the college to see me. And the minute my mother saw me she ordered me off to a hospital where I was examined by a specialist who was a surgeon.

And not a moment too soon! The doctor discovered at once that I was suffering from an attack of appendicitis, and I was rushed to the operating room. My appendix, which was about to burst, was removed and I was bedded down in a hospital room to recuperate. For the next day or so I had time to think, and I devised what to me sounded like a desperate, but workable, plot.

I wasn't afraid to tell my father—though I didn't—because I was sure that Debbie's beauty and charm would be enough to convince him. But mother was something else. And I began to think along these lines: Here am I, poor, sick Eddy, lying here in a hospital. Surely if I tell my mother about Debbie now in the presence of some of my visiting friends, she will restrain herself from any snap judgment against my bride-to-be.

So I asked my parents to summon one of my former girl friends, one of whom they had not voiced too strong an objection, and they called her to come over. When I got a chance to whisper to her for a moment, I told her my problem and begged her to act as "go-between" to ease the news to my parents.

Reluctantly, she said she'd do it "but only because you are sick." She added, "This probably isn't going to work, so don't blame me. It was your own idea."

So it was arranged that the very next day my former girl friend was to bring Debbie to the hospital with her when she came to visit me. And, while Debbie was there in the room, the former girl friend was to whisper to my mother to go out in the hall, and there my mother was to be told that "Eddy wants to marry this lovely Chinese girl who is such a good Christian and has such a lovely voice, and would make such a good wife for a young Christian minister when he starts preaching and holding special meetings." With all that endorsement, I thought, my mother will have a hard time finding reasons to say no.

Well, at first, everything went as planned. Debbie arrived with my former girl friend, and greeted me very formally and sympathetically. And then I saw the other young lady whisper to my mother, and the two of them went out into the hospital hallway.

I immediately grabbed Debbie by the hand and whispered, "Pray!" And we both closed our eyes and prayed silently for a moment that the Lord would bring this venture to a happy ending. My father was there, and he must have suspected that something was up, when he saw me holding Debbie's hand. But we said nothing. It seemed like hours before my mother and my friend came back into the room.

There was no telltale expression on my mother's face. But Mary—I think that was the girl's name—gave me a wink and a quick nod that seemed to signal everything was okay. Nothing more was said. But Mary's wink gave me a lift, and I began to chatter happily. My mother finally remarked that they had all better leave before I tired myself out talking too much.

As Debbie turned to go, I caught her eye and gave her the "okay" nod and a big smile. She winked back when no one was looking, but maintained the appearance of a circumspect young Chinese lady who was not yet aware that a "go-between" had just settled the arrangements for her marriage to me.

Later that day mother returned to the hospital alone, and we had a private talk about Debbie and our plans. With some show of face-saving hesitation she said Debbie might turn out to be a reasonably good choice for me, adding that she had been thinking, anyway, that it was about time for me to take a wife. "People don't like their ministers to be single men," she explained. "It causes talk in the church and can cause trouble."

Both families put up a good show of forgetting to "look down" at each other at our wedding. It was a happy affair, and a pleasant memory. We were married on June 25, 1957, only a few days after we graduated from college. It was Debbie's birthday.

chapter 6
Faith

I was sure that God wanted me to be a preacher. So, after Debbie and I graduated from college in June of 1957 and were married a few days later, I began to look for a good theological school. But where? And how? The best nearby were in Australia. But even "nearby" in the South Pacific was a long way, almost four thousand miles. But there were even more serious obstacles than distance. We found that we were virtually prisoners in Indonesia.

Governmental mismanagement under the Sukarno revolutionists had brought the country to the point of bankruptcy. Rigid controls on foreign exchange blocked all travel abroad by Indonesians, except in the most extreme cases of urgency. Even travel between the islands was controlled. Permits were required for imports and exports. Communications were restricted. As members of the small Chinese minority, we were suspected of both Dutch and communist leanings, and had no chance of getting any special favors from the Sukarno regime.

It looked hopeless. But we were young, optimistic, very much in love and—most important of all—we were sure the Lord wanted us to work for Him, and we knew He could find a way. So we knelt in our temporary rooms, near my parents' home, and told the Lord our troubles.

Even if our parents had been able and willing to pay our fare to Australia the exchange controls blocked them. And there was still the school tuition and living costs to consider. Also, there was the important matter of being accepted as a student at the school of our choice. Australia, at that time, was enforcing a strict quota on non-white immigrants and students.

While we waited and prayed we wrote to some of our Australian friends for information about the colleges and the costs. And I guess we also told them of our financial problems. The people we considered friends were, in the main, pastors and missionaries I had helped as an interpreter while we were in college. We felt the closest to the Reverend Reginald Wright, a Baptist pastor in Perth, and Dr. Harold Steward, a surgeon who had worked in Christian hospitals in Java between 1955 and 1957. I had come to love his family.

Within six weeks—or about the length of time it took for the mail to make the round trip—both our prayers and our letters were answered. Reginald Wright had talked to the authorities of Adelaide Bible Institute, in South Australia, and that school had granted me a scholarship to study for the L. Th. degree.

Now, under the Australian system, divinity courses from the prestigious Melbourne College of Divinity could be taken at other authorized schools, including the school to which I now had a scholarship. I was elated. But then a new thought struck me. I couldn't leave Debbie behind. And I didn't even have the money to make the trip myself. So we continued our prayers. We were sure that the Lord didn't want to separate us, after bringing us together.

A few days later, as I was walking near our home, the postman came by and handed me another letter with an

Australian postmark. With trembling hands I tore open the envelope. It was from Dr. Steward. And folded into the letter was the official student permit for Debbie. The Stewards had voluntarily sponsored Debbie when they learned that Reginald Wright was sponsoring me! I ran the half-mile home and burst in and threw my arms around Debbie. We knelt again and thanked the Lord for His kindness to us.

The way was opening, there was a scholarship waiting in Adelaide, and we were both cleared to enter the country and stay until I earned my degree. But still, there was no money to make the trip. For weeks we prayed daily that this last barrier would be lifted. Our parents agonized with us. My father, who had sold his trucks, had a bank account full of Indonesian rupiahs, but they were useless for foreign travel.

As we were praying one day, it came to me that we were not giving any evidence of our faith. So I said to Debbie, "Let's stop praying for now, and go down to the Australian consulate and start cutting through the red tape to get our visas. The Lord has done pretty well, so far. I know He's going to finish the job."

So that's what we did. It took the usual hours of waiting in bureaucratic offices. But we had the needed documents, and we finally got our visas.

Back home, we knelt again to thank God for getting us full clearance for the trip. Then I thought we were again being a little weak in our faith. So we stopped praying and asking, and rose to our feet and started praising the Lord for solving all of our problems.

As we sang together, we thought we heard a knock on the door. So we stopped for a moment, and the knock came again. Standing outside was a telegraph boy with a message from friends in Sydney: "Your tickets purchased. Pack up and come!"

The Lord kept on providing for us during our three years in

Australia. I recall one grim day when we found there was only a single shilling left in our money box, and no food in the house. What to do? Starve, or beg? No. We chose to pray. As we were on our knees we were interrupted again by a knock on the door.

This time it was a fellow student, who launched into an abject apology, as he handed us a sealed envelope. He said he had been entrusted with it several days ago, but had forgotten to give it to us. He found it in his pocket only a few minutes ago. He was very, very sorry, he said. And he hoped it was nothing important.

Inside the envelope we found twenty pounds in Australian currency, and a note that explained the money was an honorarium, in appreciation of a talk that I had given some time before at the school.

I ran into an unexpected problem when I entered the school in Adelaide. The seasons are reversed in Australia, from what they are here in the United States. Summer comes in our winter months, and winter in our summer. So the school year begins in February and ends in November. And as the school year ends, the nationwide uniform examinations are given and they get wide publicity in the newspapers.

Well, we had arrived in August, after graduating in June. I had signed up for three courses, all of them in English, which was a fairly new language for me. And the final examinations in these courses—which had started the previous February—were due within three months of the time I signed in. Some friends advised me to skip the exams and repeat the courses the next school year, beginning in February.

But I was afraid my student permit might run out before I could earn my degree if I took their advice. So I put myself on an eighteen-hours-a-day study schedule. Sympathetic fellow students filled me in on parts that I had missed. I read and reread books that had been gone through as texts while I was still in Indonesia. Debbie studied beside me, and helped by questioning me, to make sure I knew what I was reading.

On the eve of the examination, which was given at the Wesley Theological Seminary in Adelaide in November, 1957, we knelt and asked the Lord whether He really wanted me to try the exam. I realized that I might fail and that failure could endanger my scholarship. But with three months of cramming behind me, I felt the Lord would clear my mind and help me get at least a passing grade.

So I took the exam. And there followed weeks of waiting. I must admit I was nervous, despite all that the Lord had done in the past. Then, in December, the Adelaide newspapers published the names of local students who had passed the national examinations. Eagerly, we ran down the column of names. "Isn't it there? It should be right here in the 'S' section," I said, as my heart leaped in alarm. I felt a heavy sinking in my stomach, and tears of disappointment began to rise. Then I heard Debbie shriek in excitement. "Here it is," she cried. "Here it is! They've got you listed in the 'I' section, right here. Look 'Ie, Eddy.' " This was the first of a long series of incidents that finally convinced me I'd have to anglicize my Chinese name.

I got a lot more than schooling out of my stay in Australia. I also got a lot of practice preaching and making speeches. As one of the few Orientals in the school, I was sort of a curiosity. Churches invited me to tell the story of my conversion and to tell of Christian activity in Indonesia. I was invited to speak to conventions and rallies. I came to know many of the church leaders of Australia, and they gave me fatherly advice that has been invaluable. My speaking and preaching also helped to pay our expenses and improve my English. I was then a member of the Indonesian Dutch Reformed Church, which, after the revolution, had separated from the Dutch Church but retained brotherly ties and the same evangelical doctrines, and both were members of the World Presbyterian Alliance. But my Christian friends and my speaking activity were not confined to any single denomination.

For example, I had many friends among the Methodists in Adelaide. They knew of my financial stress, and they convinced the South Australia Methodist Conference that it would be a fine Christian act to lend me a helping hand.

Besides, they argued, "Eddy has a fine Christian witness," and having a Chinese preacher would help convince the world that Australians are not the racial bigots that their immigration laws make them appear to be.

So the Methodist Conference voted to make me a temporary local preacher in the Adelaide Payneham Circuit. And everywhere I preached I was received with open-hearted Christian kindness. And I hope that my experience helped to ease the immigration restrictions a few years later.

Finally, my wonderful three years in Australia came to an end. I had my L.Th. degree and a burning ambition to set the East Indies, if not the whole world, on fire for Christ. But first we had to make the trip home.

We had never traveled by ship, and this seemed like a wonderful opportunity to have that experience and, at the same time, to have a pleasant two weeks of rest aboard ship. As usual, I could not make up my mind to a complete rest, so I brought along the New Testament in Greek. I thought I would be able to get through it all before the end of the voyage.

We brushed aside warnings about the possible effects of sea travel on first-time ocean passengers, and planned only for fun and reading.

We sailed out of Sydney harbor on the beautiful new Italian liner, Neptunia, breathing the salt air deeply and enjoying the unbelievable beauty of the scene. But no sooner had we passed under the famous Sydney bridge than the ship began to roll and toss and I became deathly seasick.

Eating proved to be impossible. For several days all I could do was stay in my cabin, flat on my back. I didn't even glance in the direction of that Greek New Testament. I knew I was going to die before we reached land. And as the malady clung on, I remembered with sympathy the story of seasickness an Australian friend had told me. He had said that just before the end of his sickness his fear was not that he would die, but that he would *not* die. That gave me hope. He had survived and he said that he even enjoyed the final days of his voyage.

Just as my friend predicted, I soon began to feel better. First, I sat up and drank some clear soup. Then I ventured on deck to breathe in the fresh sea air and finally I got up the nerve to scramble up the steep stairs to the very top deck. I stood there for a while, breathing in the healing air and looking at the sky and clouds and the sea birds that dived and swooped around us. Everything looked clean and fresh and beautiful, especially this lovely ship. The sky was like a blue canopy over the dark green sea. Schools of flying fish were skimming now and then beside us. The beauty of this quiet scene made me forget, for a time, the still uncertain feeling in my stomach.

Drinking in this scene and clinging to the ship's rail, my thoughts moved on from the visible to the invisible, to the great God of the universe, the maker of all this beauty. The first chapter of Genesis seemed to pass before me, as in a movie. My heart surged up and overflowed with a deep emotion. I began to sing aloud, and to praise the Lord in a voice that was almost a shout, but was carried away by the wind. I stayed in that glorious spot for what seemed like hours, communing with the Lord of all creation.

The next morning I went again to the same place, and once again I got the feeling of semi-detachment from earthly things. Again I praised God aloud and in my heart, too, for His wonderful creation. And every day from that time on until we reached the Djakarta harbor I made the top deck my place of morning prayer and praise.

This turned out to be a significant experience in my life, and not just a passing thing. These days of joy and prayer on the top deck of the Neptunia revolutionized my way of prayer.

Up to this time I had always thought the only way to pray was to go into my room, lock the door, get on my knees, close my eyes and go through a list of requests of the Lord. But now, I suddenly realized, I could talk to God in the open air with my eyes open, even while standing or walking. This new, and to me unconventional way of prayer gave me such joy that it became a part of my lifelong routine. It has stayed with me to this day. Now, whether I am walking down the street, working in my yard, sitting in a park or driving an automobile, I can talk to God and think of His promises and His presence. Often in these mobile talks with God I am so moved that tears run down my face, and I speak aloud, though there is none but the Lord to hear me.

And occasionally the thought comes to me that I might never have found this wonderful, informal way of communing with my Maker if I had not suffered through that agonizing sea trip. I firmly believe, now, that there is value, spiritual value in suffering. My suffering on that trip led me to the secret of a way to toss aside the pressures and cares of everyday life, as if they didn't exist.

It seemed to me that everything had changed in the three years that we were away from Indonesia. After our three years in Australia, a country suffering (or possibly enjoying) under-population, the thing that struck me hardest was the masses of people everywhere we went in Indonesia. I could appreciate, at last, what I learned in school: that Java, with seventy-five million people crowded into an area about the size of New York State, was the most heavily-populated spot on earth. And I noted that among these crowds of adults there were thousands upon thousands of children, testifying to the certainty that the future in Java is likely to be as crowded, or more so, than the past.

The military seemed to be everywhere. Soldiers were in buses, in buildings, on the streets. Revolt had been spreading among the outer islands against the Sukarno regime, which held the island of Java. At the same time, the conflict between the revolutionaries and the Dutch was continuing.

I was saddened to find that many of my Dutch friends were gone. Almost all of them, in fact. All persons of Dutch ancestry had been ordered to return to the Netherlands, or to go somewhere else, but in any case to get out of Indonesia about a year after we had left. To this Dutch-oriented Chinese it hardly seemed like home with so many friendly Dutch faces gone.

About a year before our return Sukarno had scrapped his revolutionary constitution and reenacted the 1945 constitution which made our country virtually a dictatorship. Just before we landed, the new dictator dissolved parliament. He began to rule by executive decree, and took away all economic privileges of Dutch citizens. The communist-oriented dictator also abrogated his promise to pay for the interests nationalized and taken away from their Dutch owners. This amounted to about one billion dollars. Chinese citizens, suspected by Sukarno of pro-Dutch sympathies, also suffered property seizures and suffered the humiliation of being ordered to discard their Chinese names and assume new names more in line with Indonesian names.

So it was a tense and unhappy country that we came home to. The very day of our arrival a lone rebel fighter plane from one of the rebellious outer islands made a sweep over the presidential palace and fired machine guns and rockets into the building. We were riding in a bus when this happened, and were forced to get out of the vehicle and take shelter for about an hour. It seemed, on the whole, a poor time to try to bring the teachings of Jesus Christ, the Prince of Peace, to my unhappy friends and neighbors. They were living in a virtual state of war. But God had called us, and Debbie and I both were determined to plunge into our new work.

I was invited to teach in a Christian college, with the proviso that I would spend my weekends working among the young people of the Indonesian Christian Church (formerly the Dutch Reformed Church) at Tumapel. I accepted immediately. So we settled down in the nearby mountain town of Malang, Java. Later, with the consent of the church session, Debbie was employed to help with the music and the singing.

It became a lively, active church. So many university students and young professionals joined, after we started our youth work, that we started a 7:00 A.M. service on Sundays. The regular service remained at 10:00 A.M. Within a year, it was the 7:00 A.M. service that was the big one, with seven hundred or more people crowding into the sanctuary. There were little more than half that number at the 10:00 A.M. preaching.

Still later we launched a Thursday afternoon Bible study mainly for the young. And as interest rose, we also scheduled a daily prayer meeting, starting at 6:00 A.M. and running to about 6:50—timed so that students and workers could get away in time to go about their regular daily routine. (In the Asian tropics working hours normally start at 7:00 A.M. and run to noon. Then there are two hours of siesta time, before work resumes between 2:00 P.M. and 5:00 P.M.)

On Sundays, we closed the early morning prayer session at

6:45 A.M. so it would not interfere with the start of the regular 7:00 A.M. preaching service.

From the start made with this prayer meeting a Bible study group gradually formed. It met every Thursday in the church for a serious discussion of the problems of Christians and their responsibility in homes, schools and offices.

It was the eager interest in these discussions that convinced me I should give more attention to interpreting the Scriptures and how they should be applied to everyday living. Putting the Bible on a more practical level, I believe, makes Christianity more attractive, especially to those who face down-to-earth problems on a daily basis.

After a year of this kind of work, spreading my time between the college and the church, I was asked to be a full-time youth worker. The session (the body of ruling officers of the church) at the same time asked me to drop the work at the college and become a full-time member of the church staff. Up to this time I had been a sort of apprentice. So I had reached an important goal. And on my twenty-ninth birthday, November 28, 1961, I was ordained and installed as a full-fledged minister of the Indonesian Reformed Church.

My mother came to Christ shortly before I did. But my father took more convincing. He denounced us both for abandoning our ancient faith, Buddhism, and there were angry scenes and violence when mother announced her firm determination to support me in my decision to abandon the family business as a career and enter the ministry. My father angrily branded me as a thankless son for rejecting the trucking business that he had created. Things were in quite a mess at home when, suddenly, my father, who had seemed well, suffered a heart attack and was rushed to the hospital.

For a time, it looked like he was going to die. My mother and I, ignoring what we knew of his dislike for Christianity, knelt by his bed and prayed that the Lord would restore him to us. A visiting minister from Hong Kong, the late Dr. Timothy Dzao, prayed with us. We urged my father to join us, and to ask the Lord to forgive him his sins and bring him back to health.

With death staring him in the face, he finally began to weep. His obstinate spirit broke and he prayed.

The very next day when we returned to the hospital, we were astounded at the improvement in his appearance. Only a few days later the hospital said he was ready to go home. And within a matter of weeks he was as healthy and robust and active as ever. On the day he left the hospital he was carrying a copy of the Chinese Bible under his arm. He had been studying the Book of Ecclesiastes, and he said it almost seemed familiar to him, because it was so similar to the teachings of Confucius.

My father was deeply and genuinely converted to Christianity, and was so grateful for the restoration of his health that he, also, decided to enter the Christian ministry. He sold his trucking business and returned to school. There it became obvious that he did not have a great future as a preacher, but it was discovered that he had a great gift for learning and speaking foreign languages. So he chose to study to become an interpreter for visiting preachers and missionaries in Java.

He lived for ten years after that heart attack. And before he died he had become one of the most popular and most sought-after interpreters in Indonesia. And his reputation for interpreting sermons from English to Indonesian or from Chinese to Indonesian was spread far beyond the borders of Indonesia by the ministers of the gospel he had helped.

chapter 7

The Harvest

The rain came down like a thundering waterfall! Roads were flooded and impassable. Streams and rivers overflowed. The water rose to bridge level and then began to flow across the tops of bridges, Nobody could remember any rain like it. Such a cloudburst! Such a torrential downpour! And still it came down, hour after hour.

To me, an eager young preacher assigned to my very first effort as an evangelist for the Reformed Church of Indonesia, it looked like the work of the devil. As I looked out the window at the rising flood that first morning in Tasikmalaya, the West Java town where I was supposed to begin a series of five evangelistic meetings that very evening, I felt a wave of bitter disappointment sweep over me. "Defeated," I thought. "Defeated by the devil even before I get a chance to start my ministry."

Debbie was with me, and we met with the church officers to discuss the outlook and decide whether or not it might be best to cancel the service for that night. We seemed pretty much in agreement that it would be futile to expect people to come to church when most of them were at the moment trying furiously to protect their homes and property against damage from flooding. So we swallowed our disappointment and knelt together and suggested, politely, to the Lord that if He had the time and if it was His will, we would appreciate it if He would stop this awful rain, if not today, then maybe in time for tomorrow's meeting. It was a childish sort of prayer. We were really saying, "After all, Lord, we are here to do your work and it seems the least you can do is give us decent weather."

We rose from our knees with heavy hearts, the rain still drumming on the roof. But we had some second thoughts about canceling. The services had been widely advertised, and if even a few came out, in spite of the terrible weather, the least we could do was have the church open, and stand ready to go ahead with the preaching service. Besides, we thought, a little bit of hymn singing, and a song or two from Debbie, might help to lift the spirits. So we went ahead with preparations.

I was deeply engrossed with my sermon, and with Bible reading, when I began to sense a change. It was about three o'clock in the afternoon, and for a moment, as I struggled to shift my mind from my studies to what was going on around me, I couldn't place what it was that had distracted me. And then it struck me! The rain had stopped! At least, I couldn't hear it any more! I walked quickly to the window. It was true! No more rain! Not a drop was falling! The clouds were breaking up, and the sun was beginning to send needles of light across the soggy landscape.

Water on the streets was flowing off rapidly. The Lord had heard our childish prayers and stopped the storm! So we knelt again with joy leaping in our hearts and gave thanks and praise to our all-powerful creator.

The word spread quickly through the city. "It was a miracle," they were saying. "The pastor and the evangelist prayed, and the rains stopped. How lucky we are that the Christian meeting was tonight! We might have been flooded out of our homes. This is a mysterious thing. But it has happened before our eyes."

The service was to start at six o'clock. By five o'clock the sanctuary was filled to capacity, and still they came. At 5:30, when we came to the church, we had to push our way through the crowd on the parking lot and in the streets. Inside the sanctuary, even the aisles were packed. Someone had called the police to clear the streets for traffic. Amplifiers were produced from somewhere, so the people outside could hear. There were overflow crowds and bright skies, and that's the way it went for a full five days.

The meeting was the talk of the town. The wonder of God who had stopped that unnatural downpour and transformed the climate of the entire district for a week so His messenger could bring the gospel to the people of Tasikmalaya. What I had mistakenly thought was a work of the devil turned out to be the beginning of a miracle that brought thousands of non-believers to the meetings, and led many of them to accept Jesus as their Savior.

The miracle of the stopping of the rain at Tasikmalaya transformed the first crusade of an unknown evangelist into a triumphal harvest for the Lord, throughout the two months we were on the road. I had been assigned to this 1961 effort by the East Java Synod, which had appointed me to the Committee for Evangelism soon after my ordination. The area assigned to me covered the three provinces of East, Central and West Java.

There was another happening during this first crusade that I think might be classified as a miracle. We traveled by train, and at one point we passed through a jungle region where outlaws had been attacking trains and robbing and sometimes killing the passengers.

Only a week or so before we passed that way, a train had been stopped and several passengers died in the battle between the outlaws and the troops that always rode the trains as guards at that time.

We peered out the windows of the coach nervously as our train moved into the outlaw area. We watched the jungles for the first sign of hostile action. Troops aboard our car stood on the platforms at each entrance door, with rifles cocked and ready. Windows were ordered tightly closed, despite the heat and the humidity, and the atmosphere inside the cars grew stuffy and sickening.

The train crept on at what seemed like an unnecessarily low speed, and we unconsciously moved our bodies to try to make it go a little faster. Then, there was a screeching, scraping sound, and the train jerked to a halt. We waited breathlessly, expecting shouts and gunfire. The troops in our car knelt and peered out the windows. A trainman came running through the cars, and called over his shoulder as he ran that it was "nothing." He said there was "trouble with the brakes. We will be going in a moment."

But there we sat for nearly an hour. A stalled train, filled to capacity with passengers, was an invitation to banditry and robbery. But there was not a movement, not a sound from the trees that bordered the tracks so closely on either side.

Finally, to our great relief, there was a shrill whistle from the locomotive and we began to move again. We said a silent prayer of thanksgiving.

But it was only a few days later that we read in the newspapers that another train had been stopped in that same dangerous region, and scores of passengers had been killed. All had been robbed of their possessions. Surely, we felt, the Holy Spirit had protected us, as we sat there in a train that was disabled and could not have escaped.

The second series of meetings in my "rookie" tour as an evangelist in 1961 was held in a big Methodist church in Jakarta, a city of more sophisticated university students, government officials and professionals. In my heart I was certain that these educated people would soon see through my thin veil of theological learning, and would leave me with a lot of empty seats after their first experience under my preaching.

But in my anxiety to do my best to be eloquent and persuasive I forgot the great truth that the messengers of God should always keep in mind: It is the Holy Spirit working with you, who brings the souls to Christ. You may stutter and stumble and feel you have failed. But if the Holy Spirit is with you, you cannot fail.

The story of the stopping of the rain had arrived ahead of me, and the large Methodist sanctuary was packed the first night. After the meeting I thought, "They've heard my simple sermon now. There'll be plenty of empty seats tomorrow." But the second night every seat was filled, and there was little standing room left! And for the final three nights the city fathers sent police to keep the streets clear and traffic moving through the crowds that listened to the services standing outside the church.

Our performance was never altered. I had prepared only five sermons, one for each night at each city. Debbie sang, our musicians played and there were prayers and announcements until everyone was assembled. And then I preached. And the response always overwhelmed me. I knew then and I know now that the thousands who made decisions for Christ in those meetings could not have been so convicted merely by the simple sermons of my beginning years. The Holy Spirit was at work in Indonesia, and Eddy Swieson was only "fronting" for

Him.

Forewarned by the unexpected enthusiasm in our first two cities, we took the precaution of warning the police in advance when we reached Semarang, in Central Java. We told them we expected a large crowd and asked for "an officer" to keep order.

The officers were polite, but it was obvious they didn't think there would be enough interest in a Christian revival in that city to warrant police help. They said they would surely come if needed, leaving the clear impression they were going to forget it. But by the second night, after a traffic snarl caused by our crowds the first night, the police turned out in force.

At the city of Solo, the sophisticated cultural center of Central Java, and again in the overwhelmingly Moslem city of Bondowoso there was evidence the Holy Spirit was moving. Hundreds of Moslem believers accepted Christ, and on the last night the local Christians and many of the new converts begged us to continue the meetings there. "The revival has only begun here," they said. "Stay with us and we can win this whole province for Christ!" But we were soldiers of the church, and we had our marching orders. Meetings were set and advertised and ready to start the following week in Surabaya, the capital city, so we reluctantly and tearfully closed our final prolonged meeting with song and praise and prayers of thankfulness. And then we packed and moved on.

Surabaya—we will never forget that experience! It was a fitting climax to an unexpectedly glorious crusade.

Our meetings were to be held in the biggest Reformed church in the capital city. But several hours before the starting time the church officers came to me in breathless amazement.

"The sanctuary is filled already!" they reported. "And now people are gathering in the parking lots. They have brought chairs and pillows to sit on. We must find larger quarters. Do you mind if we rent the municipal auditorium? The police and the fire inspectors are complaining already that the church is over-full."

But it was too late to change locations the first night, and we sang and preached to a packed sanctuary and to many hundreds outside by amplifiers. And the second night even the bigger municipal auditorium was filled and hundreds more listened outside. This was heady stuff for a young preacher. Debbie was always there to dampen my ego when I might make some remark that hinted I was beginning to take the credit for all this excitement.

"Was it you who stopped the rain at Tasikmalaya?" she would ask with a sly smile. And that was enough. I got the message.

The Surabaya police, incidentally, were getting a little irritable by the time our meeting closed. If ours had been an Islamic gathering they would have controlled the crowds without comment. That's because ninety-five percent of the populace were Moslem and so were the police. But there was nothing in the book of police regulations that called for assisting at meetings of Christians. There weren't supposed to be enough Christians in the city to disrupt traffic. And that is the reason why we were so excited. We knew that the majority of those who came to our meetings must be non-believers, because there were hardly that many members in all the city's Christian churches combined. And when the final meeting ended, the people were reluctant to leave. The local pastors begged us to continue. But we could not.

I still remember our departure from the crowded municipal auditorium that final night. It was almost like the departure of a Hollywood star or a high political figure. I was escorted from the hall by police to a waiting car. With Debbie sitting beside me, the car crept at a snail's pace through the crowded street, with police going ahead of us to open the way.

Inside, Debbie and I waved to the people as we worked our way through. And the thought flashed through my mind, "Lord, look at us! Here we are, waving and taking credit for a job that you have done! Dear Lord, forgive us!"

Before we left for home, the local pastors made one more effort to continue the meetings beyond the five days. They told us they could get the Surabaya stadium for a week, if we would stay. It was the ultimate compliment to me, and I prayed about it. But, all along, I knew in my heart that it was best to "stop while we were ahead," as the gamblers say. I had preached all of my five sermons. A sixth would have to be put together in a hurry. And we were both tired from two months of travel. My faith in God did not waver, but I had much less faith in my own ability to continue. So we brought our first memorable crusade to a close.

The next year, 1962, the Committee on Evangelism assigned us to a second crusade over the same route. And the memory of the crowds that came in 1961 led to a lot of exaggerated advertising by the local people. It was in 1962 that they started, without consulting me, billing this unworthy young preacher as "the Billy Graham of Indonesia."

It was an undeserved compliment, and I knew it, but the local pastors argued that to link my name with Billy Graham's would have the magical effect of drawing even larger crowds.

As a matter of fact, it did work out exactly that way. And I want to thank Dr. Graham for the use of his name. I'm sure the Lord will give him a large share of the credit for the harvest of souls in our second crusade.

While I was in Surabaya on the first crusade I met some of my old high school buddies who had known me in school, when I was a devout Buddhist.

"When in the world did you switch religions?" they asked, slapping me on the back. Some of them even came to the meetings. Out of curiosity, I suppose.

"How did a rascal like you ever turn into a saint and a prophet in such a short time?" I was asked. I was not sure that I liked that comment, and I stiffly reminded them that it was twelve years ago that we were in high school. Besides that, I did not claim to be either saint or prophet.

I was sorry later that I had replied that way, because it dawned on me that my sudden appearance as a Christian evangelist might help bring about the conversion of some of my old friends. One of them, I know, did accept Christ. He told me, "People come to me now to ask about you because they have heard I knew you in school. How can I convince them what a mischief-maker you were? How can I even tell them that? They won't believe it. They'll just think I was bragging when I said I knew you, and was lying all the time."

He laughed as he walked away. And then he added, "Look for me at your meetings next year. I'll be there." He was. And he was, by then, already a Christian.

Pastors who took part in Eddy's ordination November 28, 1961 at Malang, East Java. He pastored the Malang church for two years, 1960-1962.

Eddy (far right) presiding at a conference of professors at Petra University, Surabaya, Java, during a visit in 1973.

Eddie in his doctoral robe, 1975.

Eddie and his wife, Deborah, on the campus of American University, Washington, D.C., the day he received his doctorate from Wesley Theological Seminary.

Left to right: Eddie, Rini Tan, and Deborah. This photograph was taken in January, 1975 during Rini Tan's visit to Washington after her husband's death.

The Swieson family at Montgomery County (Md.) Courthouse on the day they became naturalized citizens, October, 1970. With them is Judge Kathryn J. Shook, who presided at the ceremony.

Fourth Presbyterian Church. This picture shows the front of the sanctuary (just enlarged and already too small) with the Sunday school building showing in part on the left.

Dr. Richard C. Halverson, pastor of the Fourth Presbyterian Church.

Eddy greets one of the Ambassador class members and her visiting father.

Eddy at the Sunday morning session of the Ambassadors career-age class. Membership has grown so large that the class must now meet (as in this picture) at an auditorium attached to the new quarters of the Bethesda-Chevy Chase Rescue Squad, which is located a mile away from the church.

Eddy and Dr. Halverson in Halverson's church office.

chapter 8
New Horizons

While I was in Australia I joined the Overseas Christian Fellowship because I thought it would be nice to continue our Christian contacts with the young men and women who were studying beside us there. What I could not possibly have known, at the time, was that this simple decision would lead to a major change in the course of my whole life, and in the direction of my ministry.

It was in October of 1962, almost three years after we graduated from the Bible college in Adelaide, that I began to receive letters from other Asian Christians in various countries—preachers whom I had known as graduate students in Australia—inviting me to speak at Christian conferences in a number of different countries in Southeast Asia and other parts of the Far East. Of course, it was impossible for us to travel abroad from Indonesia on our own decision because of the strict control of foreign exchange. Fortunately, our friends abroad were aware of these financial barriers, so each invitation was accompanied by an offer to pay travel costs.

Debbie and I became more and more excited over the prospect of "escaping" for a time the severe restrictions on travel by Indonesians. We also were elated over the chance to see our friends again, and to see what Asian Christians were doing in other countries. So we looked over our invitations and found it was possible to schedule them, one after another, over a period of six months. Thus we started, in October of 1962, a six-months trip that was to change our lives.

Preparing for the trip, I polished my English by listening to the Voice of America program in "special (simple) English," broadcast daily from Washington. I listened to it religiously because I was afraid my English was evaporating from lack of use. If I had known that within one year I would be broadcasting from Washington, I'm afraid I would have died from eager anticipation. Because it was during those hours of listening to VOA that I began to dream of the vast harvest of souls that could be brought into Christ's kingdom if a Christian message could be broadcast to my country, like that VOA message, which, of course, was a program aimed at "selling" America, not Jesus Christ. But I brushed aside the dream. It was impossible. Yet, in the back of my mind I was convinced that radio would be the perfect solution to the difficulties facing Christian missionaries and preachers in Indonesia.

Under the communist-dominated Sukarno regime travel, even between the islands, was all but impossible. Many were in rebellion against Sukarno. Mail was being censored. All tapes found in the mail were being confiscated. Travel permits were hard to get, and even harder to get if you happened to be of Chinese extraction.

The first stop on our Asian odyssey was the Federation of Malaysia and Singapore, where English was spoken. There I could speak and preach without interpretation, thanks to the Voice of America. (By coincidence, the VOA broadcaster at that time was Forrest Boyd, who later became a close friend as a member of Fourth Church.)

We moved ahead on schedule, keeping all our engagements to lecture at theological schools and colleges, to preach at Christian crusades and to attend church conferences. Our schedule took us through Thailand and then to Hong Kong. It was in Hong Kong where the shape of things to come was first revealed to us. But we did not think of it at the time as a prophetic occurrence. What happened was this: We met the Hong Kong manager of the Far East Broadcasting Company, a missionary whose job it was to get the Christian message into Red China. He seized the opportunity of our visit—noting that we were Chinese—to ask us to make some tapes of sermons and songs for his radio station.

I had to explain to him that it was Debbie who was fluent in Chinese, and that I had learned what I knew of it from her. So it came about that Debbie was the star of these early efforts of the Swieson family as Christian broadcasters. She taped several talks in Chinese, and sang religious songs. They were broadcast after we left, but the experience was exciting. And it couldn't have come at a better time. For at our next stop, in Manila, we were invited to have a look at the studios of the Far East Broadcasting Company, a missionary institution. By fortunate "coincidence" Robert Bowman, president of the company, was also there on a visit. He had heard of our successful Indonesian evangelistic tours. And he began urging us to switch to a radio ministry. And before we knew what was happening, he had talked us into thinking seriously about making some experimental Christian broadcasts for his station. He was a high-pressure salesman.

He explained it was impossible to get tapes to or from Indonesia. They were being "lost" in the mails, on orders of the censors.

"The only way to get the gospel to your country," he said, "is by radio. When we go in on the air waves, we can reach every one of your three thousand islands. There is no way to put up a wall to keep us out."

He exhorted us to be brave and step into a new broadcasting career without fear. He guaranteed that if we would agree to supply his station with tapes in the native Indonesian language he would see to it they were broadcast to the people who need the message of Christ the most.

It was tempting! So tempting! We even talked of abandoning the rest of our trip and switching to a broadcast ministry, right then and there. In my dreams about broadcasting I had always counted on a long, hard struggle to get a start. And here I was having such an offer laid in my lap. And I was hesitating! But every time we leaned toward accepting his offer at once, the voices of our conscience reminded us that we had made some promises to the friends who were paying for our trip. Should we break our promises? No, that would not do.

So, in the end, Debbie and I agreed only to make a dozen experimental tapes while we were there, to see if we could do it, and to see if the station liked what we did, and what the reaction of the listeners would be.

Debbie sang at the opening of each taped program. I spoke briefly, usually about ten minutes. Then the program closed with some more singing by Debbie. For me, the toughest part was to keep from talking too long. I ran overtime on several tapes, and we had to do them over again. They had to fit exactly into the number of allotted minutes, and not a second longer. It was great discipline for me. It forced me to organize my thoughts better than I had ever managed to do before, and to be more precise in expressing them.

Finally we completed a dozen tapes, each about fifteen minutes long. We handed them over to the station staff the day we left, and they told us they would start broadcasting them at once.

So we left for a rather lengthy visit to Japan to carry out our promises, and within a few more days we had all but forgotten the twelve taped Christian broadcasts that we had left behind in Manila.

We were genuinely surprised a few weeks later, to get a phone call from Bob Bowman at our hotel in Tokyo. He had just arrived there from Manila, and told us he had terrific news! "How soon can I talk to you?" he said. "How about right now? If you can't come to my hotel, I'll get to yours."

The urgency in his voice was exciting in itself. We told him we would come to his hotel, as soon as we changed our clothes.

In the lobby of his hotel, the Marunouchi, Bob gave us his exciting report. Our tapes were a smashing success, he said. They were so successful, he went on, that the station was being swamped with mail, praising the programs and demanding to know the identity of this new preacher and his wife. "You've just got to join us now," he urged. "It's not just Bob Bowman speaking now, it's the radio audience of all of southeastern Asia! They want to hear you both. Debbie's singing was a hit. She drew many listeners who would not have tuned in to an all-talk show."

Still we wavered. We explored the possibilities in depth. Bob took the historical view. Because of the unfortunate restriction of liberties by Sukarno, he argued, we have a wonderful opportunity for a massive ministry by radio, at this particular time.

"Don't let this chance slip by," he pleaded. "There is no other way to bring Indonesia to Christ, under the rule of a dictator." He was giving right back to me the very arguments that I had been making to myself.

I knew that if I returned to my country, my ministry would be confined to the island of Java. I was sure, too, that there was a vast audience of owners of shortwave sets in the islands. And Bob put in, too, that there were millions in Singapore and the Malay states and Brunei, and in other islands near Indonesia who speak the Indonesian Malay language.

He explained that the way they judged the total number of listeners was by the number of letters received. Because of the widespread poverty in the area, they figured that one letter received represented one thousand listeners. The other nine hundred and ninety-nine were either too poor to pay the postage—which cost as much as a plate of rice—or too uneducated to write.

Still I hesitated. I remembered the thrill of preaching to the vast, overflowing audiences on the Java crusades and seeing and hearing them with my own eyes and ears as they gave their lives to Christ.

I knew that I would disappear from public view and even my name would cease to be known, if I stayed for long in the radio business. No longer would my friends kiddingly call me "the Billy Graham of Indonesia." On the air I would be only "a voice without a name." Even without Bob's assurance that God would know me, even if the world didn't, it was a difficult decision to make.

It was, in effect, obeying a call to anonymity. I would like to be famous and admired, as much as anyone, as any other human being. But I knew, too, that it would cripple my radio ministry if I gave my name, for if the millions in Asia who despise the Chinese for their business talents and prosperity, heard that I was one of the despised, clannish Chinese, they would turn me off, and probably turn Christ off, too.

There was no chance of getting permission to make Christian broadcasts from stations inside Indonesia. They were all government-owned and run. And they were dominated by the ruling pro-communist faction.

The thought that I would have to leave my country, and possibly never go back again, brought a wave of sadness in the midst of the exciting thoughts about this new career. And there was a special sadness for me, alone, in the thought that I might never see my beloved foster mother again—the mother to whom I owed my life and health.

As I wavered at this point, the Lord led me to a meeting with Dr. Gordon Chapman, a Presbyterian missionary and a great man of God, who promptly joined the others in urging me to make the change, to forget the anonymity of the job and the obscurity that was necessary. "Remember," he said, "God will know what you are doing."

So after a session of prayer, Debbie and I finally said yes.

Then, as we pondered where to have our base of operations, it was Dr. Chapman who suggested the Fourth Presbyterian Church, in Washington, D.C. He gave two reasons for the choice. First, because the pastor there was the Rev. Richard C. Halverson, a man with a worldwide vision of the ministry of the gospel, a man with a special stake in that ministry, through his leadership of the World Vision movement. Second, also a very important reason, because Fourth Church already had a radio ministry of its own. It was broadcasting its Sunday morning services, through a fully equipped studio in the church itself. And the studio was not used during the week and could be borrowed by me.

We checked all these ideas with our missionary friends, and got unanimous approval. After that, our minds were made up. The United States was the place to go.

But how to get there? It was seven thousand miles to the Pacific coast, and more than three thousand miles further to Washington. So we had a financial problem now. But we went ahead, gathering letters of introduction to Dr. Halverson and others. Then, as we thought we'd better start consulting the Lord about money problems, Debbie came through with the solution! "I will ask my brother, Ban," she said.

Now Ban, of all the eleven brothers and sisters in Debbie's big family, was my favorite. When there was no father to give Debbie away at our wedding, brother Ban stood in. He was not a Christian at that time, but he was the only one of Debbie's non-Christian family members who always asked me to pray at mealtime. He said he admired my choice of a life work. At this important juncture, he was operating an import-export business overseas, well beyond Sukarno's exchange controls.

Brother Ban came through in our money crisis, as he had helped in other troubles. He came through fast and with all the financial help we needed. We hadn't even had time to think of a possible alternative source of help when his money order came. And with it he sent his wishes for success in our new ministry and our new country. He said his prayers would go with us.

Ban died of a heart attack behind the wheel of a car in Australia in 1975. I think he was a Christian at the end. I think that even while he was still a sort of Buddhist, so far as the public was concerned, he was following the teachings of Christ. When his wife, Kim, phoned us of his death from Australia, I told her that I thought we would meet him again, in heaven. He was truly a good, kind, compassionate and charitable man. I'm sure that Jesus loved him.

As for us, Ban's telegram removed the last doubt and the final barrier. We took off for the United States firm in our faith we were doing what God wanted us to do.

chapter 9

The Voice
without a Name

Our soaring hopes and expanding ambition to launch a radio ministry that would shake the Oriental world were suddenly deflated when we landed in California. What a country! The confusion of roaring expressways, flashing red and green lights, signs that said "walk" when we wanted to stop for a moment and look, then flashed to "don't walk" just as we got ready to move on. People rushing past in both directions, obviously in such a hurry we didn't dare stop them to ask directions. Buildings that poked through the clouds, and taxi fares even higher. It was all frightening and made us feel very small and a little lonely. We wondered, that first day in America, if we would ever feel at home in this land of, what seemed to us, deliberately organized disorder, or carefully created chaos. How to do God's work in such confusion?

But, as we flew east, America came into focus. There was a sweep and grandeur in the mountains, the deep gorges, the deserts and plains, and the glistening little cities that seemed to be passing in parade as we passed over. The beautiful young hostesses were extra kind to us. We had expected to be shunned. We had heard of the prejudice against Orientals. So it was a happy surprise when an executive-looking Caucasian leaned across the aisle to offer a good view of the Grand Canyon from his side of the airplane. Though we never spoke without first being spoken to, we found ourselves telling about our prospective new work to several others on the cross-country flight. One of them confided that he, too, was active in church work and we talked about the difficulties of the churches in revolutionary Indonesia. Our hearts quickly warmed to these friendly people. But still we wondered. Have we made a mistake in choosing to work in America? It is so big. And we are so small.

All doubts vanished when we landed in Washington. We were greeted with a friendly handshake and a brotherly hug. Dr. Halverson had been briefed in detail about our plans. He told us, at once, that the radio room at the church was ours to use. He wiped out the last vestiges of our worry when he told us the church wanted to sponsor and support us as its own missionaries! And he took us to temporary quarters that he had prepared for us. Suddenly we knew that we were at home! We felt that we were swimming in an ocean of Christian love! We wept a little, out of pure happiness. And then we knelt and asked the Lord to forgive our doubts and fears and to strengthen our faith.

After that happy start, things got better and better. At the studio on our first day we found an expert producer—a real perfectionist—Edward Walker, of a local radio station, waiting to work with us. He had music ready for the early tapes. One of his favorites was Ted Smith, Billy Graham's pianist, whose recordings soon became popular in Asia through our programs. Glenn Kirkland, a scientist at Johns Hopkins University, lent us his expertise at radio engineering. Finally, by September, 1963, we were ready to start.

At first, we put together two taped programs a week, and sent them by air mail to the Far East Broadcasting Company station in Manila. They were beamed to areas where Indonesian and Chinese were understood.

The staff in Manila was swamped with mail from listeners. So at the end of the first six months we added a third program weekly. And we started a question-and-answer program, concentrating on the questions most often asked about this strange new religion called Christianity.

We never gave our Washington address on the air. And we never told our listeners that it was Eddy Swieson talking. But we were tempted. I guess I am as fond of praise and fame as anyone, and it was tough to remain anonymous with so many listeners asking for autographed photos, or at least the identity of what they began to call "the voice without a name."

Officials of Asiatic governments wrote on fine stationery, asking who was doing the preaching. University students sent fan letters to the unknown voice written on lined notebook paper. Others, too poor to buy writing pads, sent letters written on pieces of brown paper bags. The pressure grew. I was tempted again and again to give my name maybe just once—and to tell them how the programs reached them from Washington.

But I prayed about it, and the Lord laid a steadying hand on my shoulder. I was reminded, again, of the prejudice that millions in Asia hold against my race, and also against the Dutch Reformed Church that was my alma mater in the body of Christ.

The Lord seemed to be saying, "Steady, Eddy. You're doing just fine. Keep on as you are. Maybe the world doesn't know you, but I do."

To attract the more sophisticated listeners, we "baited" our programs with interludes of classical music, and religious and popular songs, both before and after the sermon. And we also deliberately complimented our listeners' intelligence by using English words now and then, somewhat Indonesianized, as if to say to them that we were sure they were smart enough to know what the words meant. Sukarno used the same tactic in his rise to power.

By trial and error, and by reading the mail, we found what the listeners liked in music, and what interested, or puzzled them most about the gospel. And we emphasized these things.

After three years of this we made a listener survey. It was clear that "the Indonesian News of Hope" programs had "arrived." Our audience was estimated at no less than three million.

Between September of 1963 and early 1970 when the final program was taped, we had preached and sung and played music for our vast congregation more than four hundred times—as recorded on four hundred separate tapes.

And now and then—probably twenty or thirty times—Debbie had starred in her own taped programs in Mandarin Chinese, both preaching and singing for listeners in mainland China.

But the end of the taping did not end the broadcasts. With letters of enthusiasm still pouring in, the Manila station started rerunning the tapes it had on hand. And for six years after the last tape was produced in 1970, the "voice without a name" spoke out on its regular weekly schedule from Manila. No one seemed to notice, at least they didn't complain, that they had heard the same words some years before. There were enough tapes so that it was not necessary to repeat any one program oftener than every two or three years.

Finally, the Manila broadcasters called for help.

"We still have your program on our schedule," they wrote. "It is being beamed to Indonesia and Malaysia. The musical and question-and-answer tapes have been taken off because we are not getting any new tapes from you. But we are planning to continue the sermon and musical programs on our Indonesian schedule for the 1976 season. You will note that all are on three prime times, with the family as the intended audience. All have been aired several times now, and we certainly need some fresh programs to keep us going."

To add a little pressure to their argument, the broadcasters sent the contents of a few sample letters for me to read. A youth from Malaysia wrote, "At last I have found salvation! Jesus Christ came to save me and died for my sins. What a wonderful Savior! FEBC has saved countless souls, and I am one of them. I thank you very much."

Another listener, from Pakistan, said, "Being a Muslim I should not care to listen to your programs, but this is not the case with me. In my own views I have the same respect for Christianity, so I am listening regularly to the sweet voice of Jesus. I have gained a lot of knowledge through your different programs. I like the programs about the Lord most. I am very eager to know more, and in detail, about Jesus."

I read these letters with mixed feelings of joy and sadness. Joy because my broadcasts were still bearing fruit. Sadness because in my heart I knew it was impossible, and maybe even unnecessary, to produce a new series of tapes of the voice without a name. Even while still broadcasting I had gratefully accepted the offer to become assistant pastor of the Fourth Presbyterian Church. And when the period of broadcasting came to an end, Dr. Halverson had asked me to take on the heavier task of associate pastor, which involved more preaching and a busier schedule of Bible teaching. How could I add a schedule of broadcasting to this?

But there is still another reason why I feel the voice without a name should now be allowed to fall silent. There is now a fast-growing crop of active, eager young Christian ministers in Indonesia. Under the Suharto government there are few restrictions on travel, freedom of speech and freedom of worship. The time of oppression is past. The word of God now can be preached face to face with the people who need to hear it.

So the voice without a name will not return. And to preserve whatever good the programs did, in their day, the voice will never be identified.

On a recent anniversary of the founding of the Indonesian State, I was invited to the customary reception given at the embassy in Washington. I arrived a little late, and was met at the door by the ambassador. He scolded me good-naturedly for working too hard and too long, then he took me by the arm and introduced me to a circle of newly arrived guests, recent arrivals from Indonesia.

One of them, a businessman in Washington to push Indonesian exports, looked me over curiously.

"Isn't it rather remarkable that you, an Oriental, are preaching at this big American church?" he asked.

I thanked him for what I knew he intended as a compliment even though there seemed to be undertones of doubt about the fitness of an Oriental to handle such a job.

"The Lord has been very good to me," I said. "He has given me opportunities for service to Him far above and beyond what I ever dreamed would be possible."

The man looked at me in a strange way, again, and said, with a question in his voice: "We must have met before. I don't recall your face, but your voice is very familiar to me. I'm sure we must have talked together. Possibly by phone, and not too long ago. I'm pretty good at remembering voices, although I don't always attach names to them."

"No," I replied. "I don't think we have ever met. I have been living in America now for more than a decade, and I have become an American citizen. So, if this is your first visit to the United States, as you say it is, then it surely is not possible that we have met. There must be another voice somewhere in Indonesia that sounds like mine." I shook his hand and wished him well and moved on to another group of guests.

But when I turned and looked back, the traveling Indonesian businessman was still looking after me with a puzzled expression.

A few moments later, while I was talking with an American friend, there was a gentle tap on my shoulder, and there, standing behind me with a triumphant smile on his face, was my Indonesian businessman.

"I've got it!" he burst out. "I know who you are! You are the 'voice without a name.' You are the Indonesian News of Hope broadcaster! That must be it. You are a minister, and the News of Hope broadcaster was a preacher of sermons. Your voice and his voice sound exactly the same. I have listened often. I like your music. That girl who sings. Who is she? Is she your wife, or maybe your daughter? Now, am I right? I know it has been a secret, but I think I have solved it. Tell me, are you the voice without a name?"

I smiled and tried to put a surprised and doubtful sort of look on my face, but I couldn't hold it. I finally broke into laughter.

"You would make a great detective," I said. "Yes, I will confess, now that you have cornered me. After all, I am a Christian minister and I cannot tell outright lies, and I should not even give false impressions. I was the voice, several years ago."

"Was?" he said, with a question obviously coming. "But I heard you only last month, before I left Indonesia on this tour. Is there now an imposter taking your place?" Then, after a moment of pondering, he asked, "If you have been living in America so long, when did you do your broadcasting? I suppose

91

we are listening to some of your old records now.''

So I told him the whole story, of how we had moved to America because of oppression that blocked the sending of tapes out of Indonesia for broadcasting back to our country. And I explained that "the voice" had always come from Washington, D.C., never live from Manila. And I assured him that the lovely lady whose singing he admired was my wife, not my daughter.

"But why all the hush-hush secrecy about it?" he asked. "Why didn't you announce your name? By now you would be famous all over the Orient. You are a pretty good preacher. Were you ashamed of your job? Or didn't your boss allow you to give your name?"

I chuckled a bit and then nodded: "You have guessed it again," I said. "My boss thought it best for me to remain anonymous." In my thoughts I silently asked the Lord to forgive me for skirting the truth and calling Him "boss."

And then I added, "I was born in Indonesia, but I am Chinese. And you know how many of our people have unkind opinions of us. If I had given you my Chinese name, instead of only the sound of my voice, would you have listened to me? Would all the mixed nationalities and religions of our homeland have listened? To a native Indonesian, probably. To an Indonesian with a Chinese name, no! The 'boss' was obviously right in keeping me out of the picture."

"Humpf," my friend commented. "I'd never work for a boss like that!"

I shook his hand, as I started to move off, and replied, "I think you would."

chapter 10

The Challenge

It was after I had been working two years in Washington at my broadcasting job that I received a telephone call that left me stunned.

It came from Dr. Halverson, and it was brief and to the point. "Eddy," he said, "I want you to become assistant pastor of Fourth Church."

I was so surprised that I began to stammer and stutter and choke and the words wouldn't come. And before I could pull myself together sufficiently to make an intelligent reply, Dr. Halverson interrupted with another generous offer. "It's fine with us if you want to go on with your broadcasting," he said.

When I recovered sufficiently to put together a sensible sentence of thanks, and an expression of my deep appreciation of his amazing confidence in a young Oriental who had not yet done enough preaching in English to regard himself as capable of doing it on a regular basis, the pastor cut me off again with an expression of thanks for my willingness to assume this extra burden of work.

"Burden!" I thought. "How many thousands of young preachers pray every night to be offered such a burden!"

My head was in a whirl, but I did have the presence of mind to tell Debbie, so she wouldn't think I was having some kind of a seizure. Then I sought out a chair, out of breath and limp with suppressed excitement.

This was unheard-of! An Oriental, not yet anywhere near the point of becoming an American citizen, to minister to a ninety-eight percent white Caucasian church. Will this sophisticated congregation accept me as their minister? Although I had, frankly, not seen much of the alleged prejudice against Orientals since my arrival in America, I knew it was there. And I wondered.

One of my earliest friends in the church, the late Samuel B. Coleman, was very frank in his assessment of my situation and in his advice to me. "Eddy," he said, "you're in a tough spot. This is a very affluent community. There are a lot of people here who think they are sophisticated. And there are some who really are. You are going to have to study and study and study. You must increase your knowledge and do it as fast as you can. You must sharpen your sensitivity, and always present yourself neat and clean."

I must admit I was scared. But it didn't take long for the love of this great congregation to surround and comfort me.

When the word got out that I was to be the new assistant pastor, a prominent member of the church came to my home and knocked on the door. When I opened it, he took me by the arm and led me out to the curb and presented me with the keys to the car that was parked there.

"You're going to need it," was his only comment. I did.

For the first year or more as assistant pastor I hardly dared open my mouth. I made a practice of never saying anything that anybody was likely to disagree with.

Our American friends continued to shower us with shining examples of Christian love and concern. One couple, learning that we were moving into an apartment and had little furniture, told us they wanted to take us for a drive one afternoon. They drove directly to a lovely furniture store, and told us to pick the furniture we needed for kitchen, living room and study room. And they paid for it. Later, the wife met with Debbie and they went shopping. Debbie came home with the most useful domestic tool of all, a sewing machine. It was paid for, in full, again by our friends.

I was still a member of the Indonesian Reformed Church when I arrived in Washington, but after experiencing the love and concern of the people of the Fourth Presbyterian Church, I had an overwhelming urge to join the church and thus come into closer fellowship with them.

I was told the procedure was simple. All I had to do was ask the Reformed Synod in Indonesia to transfer my membership to the Washington City Presbytery of the United Presbyterian Church in the U.S.A. Both churches are members of the World Presbyterian Alliance so, I was told, there would be no problem.

But nobody in Washington had ever tackled such a transfer before. And it was of course, my first try at it, too. So it was months before the shuttle of messages back and forth over the ten thousand miles to Indonesia and back verified that I was who I was and that the Washington Presbytery could rest assured that as an ordained minister of the Reformed Synod of Java I would preach only Jesus Christ, and Him crucified.

I had found Americans to be very self-assertive. In fact, from the viewpoint of an Oriental just in from the Orient, they seemed downright aggressive. But my fears took a positive turn. They convinced me that Mr. Coleman was right. I needed more education.

I became determined to learn everything I could cram into my head about Western thought and Western civilization. But while I was learning, I remained cautious. And I worked all sorts of

95

strategies to avoid embarrassment.

For example, if I were asked by someone to make a visit to a hospitalized member of the congregation, I would always call by telephone first and explain who I was, and ask them if they would like to have me come and talk to them and pray with them, and share the Scriptures.

The wonder of all wonders to me is that in all the years that I have ministered to this congregation, not a single door ever has been slammed in the face of this Oriental.

The only frustrations I have suffered were due to my own personal habits and disposition, my fear of being candid, my Oriental shyness and politeness.

I still remember the day that I first determined that I was being foolish in continuing this shyness and reserve. It was like putting the brakes on and slowing the process of becoming a real part of this congregation.

I was standing outside the church at the close of a service thinking of some problem, long since forgotten, and I must have been wearing an expression of concern on my face. A member of the congregation was walking past, and he took a piercing look at me, and then turned around and slapped me on the back, jolting me out of my worried trance, and he said, "Eddy, relax. We all love you."

I was determined to follow the advice of Mr. Coleman, and increase my knowledge. So I enrolled, first, at George Washington University, to study in my off hours. Later, I took courses for two years at the American University. And finally, from 1971 to May of 1974 I studied for a doctorate at the Wesley Theological Seminary in Washington. The long search for knowledge reached a high point when I was awarded my Doctorate of Ministry from the Wesley Seminary, with a specialization in the field of World Missions.

One of the most heartwarming moments of my life in America

was the first time that, as Dr. Eddy Ie Swieson, I wore in the pulpit the robe and insignia that signified the new ecclesiastical rank. Everyone in the congregation knew how long and hard I had worked and studied to earn it. And there was an unexpected spontaneous burst of applause in the packed sanctuary of that "sophisticated" 150-year-old church.

But study has been my source of "fun" most of my life. I do not consider the doctorate a goal. It's only a marker on the way to the goal. And the way that I will take to that goal will take a lifetime of study to completely cover.

Languages are my favorite study. To qualify as a Bible scholar of sufficient insight to prepare a continuing Bible study course suggested by my pastor, I have tried to acquire a working knowledge of Greek and Hebrew, and I spend as many Monday nights as possible at the Jewish Community Center, to improve my knowledge of conversational Hebrew.

In the course of my career as a student in Indonesia and Australia I have, of course, been obliged to learn Indonesian, Mandarin Chinese, Dutch and English, and I try to keep brushed up on my reading knowledge of German. Now my latest project is to master the "American" language. And this I am pursuing to put me in closer touch with the "career singles" of our church, whose problems and concerns I have found to be among the most challenging of my ministry.

Fourth Church, despite the problems of its large and growing congregation, is a church that likes to laugh. It's a happy church. And we seem to find a lot to laugh about, even in the midst of the deadly serious work for the Lord.

A recent telephone call that came to my office is a good example.

The voice on the telephone said, "Hooray for Fourth Church! You finally got yourselves a real Scottish Presbyterian preacher!

97

I just heard him on the radio, and he's great! Nothing like a good, solid Presbyterian Scot to put the gospel in words you can understand—"

The young secretary at the church interrupted politely, "Sir?" As my caller ignored the interruption and talked on, she said, again, "Sir? I think the man you are referring to is Dr. Eddy Swieson, and he—"

"Yeah, that's the name. I couldn't mistake that good Scottish accent, even before I heard the name—"

I had already pressed the button and was listening as this exchange continued.

"Well, sir," my secretary interrupted again, "Dr. Swieson is not Scottish, you see. We do think he is a fine preacher, but he is, in fact, Chinese, and he was born in Java, and brought up as a Buddhist—"

There was silence on the other end of the line, so the secretary checked to see if the caller was still there. "Sir," she began, "Sir, are you there?"

This time it was the caller who interrupted. "I don't believe it," he said. And the phone clicked dead. My secretary sighed and then, noting that I was on the line, she chuckled and said, "Eddy, that was another one." For this was not the first caller to be misled by my accent, which probably is fractured and confusing because I have spent so much of my life studying and using foreign languages.

Shortly after I came to Fourth Church I had another similar case of wrong identification. I got a call one morning from a man who said he was an Episcopalian and wanted me to officiate at his wedding. I readily agreed to do it, but I was curious as to why he wanted a Presbyterian minister when he had identified himself as an Episcopalian.

The reason he wanted me, he said, was that he had heard me preach on the radio and both he and his intended wife had enjoyed the sermon and were impressed by what I had said. And besides, he added, "the lady I am marrying is a Presbyterian."

I gave him the usual explanation of my requirement of a face-to-face meeting with the couple before the ceremony to get acquainted and to give me an opportunity to ask certain questions. He readily agreed that this was a reasonable request.

We talked by phone several more times, making the arrangements for the wedding, and finally I insisted that we set a definite date for the interview and get it over with.

So, at the appointed time there was a knock on my door. Fortunately, I was wearing my clerical collar that day, and I opened the door myself. The man shook hands with me and said that he had come to keep an appointment with Dr. Swieson.

"Well, I'm glad to see you," I said. "I'm Dr. Swieson."

Well, that man stood as if paralyzed and his face turned pale. He looked like he had seen a ghost. His jaw dropped and his eyes popped wide open, and for a moment I thought he might be having some sort of a seizure. But he came out of it quickly and we sat down and the three of us had a good talk, and got really well acquainted. But I was curious, so just as he was leaving I asked him whether he had been sick, or if not what was the matter when he first arrived for the interview. "You looked very pale and shaken," I said.

He blushed and looked at his lady and then it came out. "I almost dropped dead," he said. "You can see that I'm a Scandinavian and you have a Scandinavian name, or one that sounds Scandinavian, anyway. And you have a definite Swedish accent on the radio. I thought you were one of my countrymen, and I thought it would be nice to be married by someone from the home country. So I guess you can understand my reaction when Dr. Swieson turned out to be a

Chinese in clerical collar!"

I seem to have a weakness for getting mixed up in misunderstandings. I am frequently called upon to make hospital visits and I always wear my clerical collar and a black jacket when I do because you can't get through the doors of the intensive care unit or the baby unit unless you are obviously a minister.

One day I was called upon to make a visit to Holy Cross Hospital, which is a Catholic institution. And of course, since I was wearing the clerical collar, all the sisters and the doctors were calling me "Father."

In this case I was visiting a woman who had just given birth, and she was very insistent that I go have a look at her new baby. So I obliged and went right into the baby room, which was a little crowded with new arrivals that day. I was moving from crib to crib, peering at the name plates, when I accidentally bumped into a young man who was making the same sort of search.

"Oh, excuse me, Father," he said. "Are you looking for your baby?"

I laughed and replied, "I am looking for *a* baby, but not *my* baby."

And then it dawned on the young man what he had said. And, of course, thinking I was a Catholic priest he was covered with embarrassment and turned all shades of red. You don't say things like that to a Catholic priest. At least not yet. Their vows still prevent them from marriage.

I guess it was naughty of me not to relieve the young man of his embarrassment by confessing that I am not a priest, but a married Presbyterian, with a fine young son of my own.

Speaking of my own wife and family always reminds me of one of the most unforgettable embarrassments of my married life.

Our son, Dana, was born only after eight years of marriage. It was, indeed, a happy event, especially so since it had been so long delayed. But the events surrounding the birth were so embarrassing to me that I blush to tell about them.

When I first arrived in America and was shown through an American hospital and told of the miraculous work done by the American doctors, I acquired a great faith in their skill. I had spent a good part of my life being doctored by my mother, with substitute remedies that she concocted herself, when medicines were not available. So it gave me a secure feeling to be in a country where there was no limit to what the doctors could do, and no scarcity of medicines or equipment with which to do it.

So, when Debbie became pregnant and the doctor solemnly informed us that the baby would arrive toward the end of May or in June, I felt that my wife had no right to start complaining of birth pangs on April 12.

I told her it was probably just stomach cramps, that it couldn't be anything else. And I recall that I got her a glass of water and an aspirin and advised her to go back to sleep.

An hour later she shook me awake again.

"Eddy," she said, "I'm sure these are birth pains, and they are coming more often."

"Honey," I explained, "the doctor said 'end of May or early June' and this is only April 12. You can't be seven weeks early. It's bound to go away. So take another aspirin, or maybe a glass of milk. We've got to get some sleep."

When she got up the next morning, very early, she said she was still having pains, but I was still confident that these American doctors knew what they were talking about. So I prepared to go to the church office.

But Debbie wasn't convinced, and while I was dressing she called the doctor and he told her that she'd better come to the hospital right away. So, still laughing in a superior way and still certain it was all a false alarm I drove her to the hospital and dropped her off in front of the elevator and left for my office, with instructions for her to call me when she was ready to go back home.

I had just come back from lunch around two in the afternoon when my office phone rang. The voice on the other end of the line identified itself as the voice of a nurse on the baby ward.

"You have a fine baby son, and your wife is just fine, too," she said. Finally, I gathered my senses together and answered, "Oh!" That was all.

And all the way to the hospital, at speeds much beyond the limit, I still was suspicious that Debbie had put the nurse up to this; that it was all a practical joke on me. And I refused to believe it until I got to the hospital and felt that tiny hand grasp my finger. It was then that I wept. Tears of happiness.

But in all that excitement, I am ashamed to say, it was not until late that night that I remembered I had not yet got down on my knees and thanked the Lord Jesus Christ for giving us this precious gift.

chapter 11
Adoption

An aged man, his body painfully twisted by crippling rheumatism, was wheeled into a tiny courtroom in the local courthouse at the town of Modjokerto, near Surabaya, on the island of Java. It was September 18, 1974.

The court clerk cleared his throat, shuffled through a handful of legal papers, then looked over his glasses at the small group of men and women surrounding the wheelchair.

"Is this man Mr. Indro Imanjaja, formerly known as Mr. Ie IkDjoen, a citizen of Indonesia?" he inquired, in his customary impersonal monotone.

The old man stared a moment, with uncomprehending eyes, then nodded as he recognized his name.

"You are the father of one Eddy Ie Swieson, formerly known as Ie Swie Sing, now serving as associate pastor of the Fourth Presbyterian Church in Washington, D.C., and residing at 5405 Brookeway Drive in that city?" the clerk droned on.

The old man's eyes brightened for an instant, almost imperceptibly, at the sound of his son's name. He nodded, again, affirmatively.

"Does this man understand the significance of these

proceedings?" the clerk inquired, turning to the group standing beside the wheelchair. "Is he able to talk? Can he understand the oath and sign his name?"

"He can understand, yes, sir," one of the group replied. "But he is very weak and in much pain, and he cannot move his hands sufficiently to sign his name. But we have been told he can use his fingerprint, and it will do just as well."

"Very well," the clerk said, looking back to the papers he still held in his hands. "Then, let's proceed. Am I to understand that the son—that is, *your* son—was born on November 28, 1932 at Mojotrisno, Mojoagung, in the district of Jombang, East Java, Indonesia? We are speaking now of Mr. Eddy Ie Swieson."

The stooped, gray head peered up from the wheelchair and nodded.

"Now, according to these documents, your wife, the real mother of Mr. Eddy Ie Swieson died some years ago. Let's see, the date, I believe, is October 5, 1953. Is that correct?"

Once again, the old man nodded.

"This means, then, that you are the only surviving parent of said Eddy Ie Swieson?"

"That's right, sir," one of the accompanying group spoke up. "But may I say, again, that Mr. Imanjaja is in great pain, and it would be a kindness if we could move ahead with this as rapidly as possible."

"I understand," the clerk said, without altering his official frown. "But there are certain things that must be made clear. Judging by the age of the persons involved this case must have been pending for quite a long time, and I think we can all afford a few extra moments to make sure everything is finally in order."

Then, looking back at his papers, he went on, "These documents state that Mr. Imanjaja surrendered the above-mentioned son, Mr. Eddy Ie Swieson, to the care of Mrs.

Rini Tan, also known as Mrs. Rini Ribkah Tanutama, a housewife, residing at 241 Mojopahit, Modjokerto, East Java, Indonesia, and that she is the wife of the deceased Jusuf Pilemon Imanjaja, formerly known as Ie Ik Hwie. Is this, too, correct?"

The man in the wheelchair nodded, again. His eyes were closed.

The clerk glanced at the crippled figure and his words began to come faster.

"We must also confirm that Mrs. Rini Ribkah Tanutama and Mr. Jusuf Pilemon Imanjaja both obtained these new names, based on the decision of the presidential cabinet of the Republic of Indonesia, Number 127/U/Kep. 12/1966, accepted and approved by the mayor of the city of Surabaya on August 5, 1967, Registered Number 3911/Gt/Nm/Komad/1967L, which has been shown to me."

Looking over his glasses toward the wheelchair, he turned quickly back to his reading even before the old man was able to nod his approval.

"The death certificate of Mr. Jusuf Pilemon has been shown to me, so we can skip the certification there. But now, this is an important point: In addition to expressing his consent, the one who appears before me here today," he nodded in the direction of the wheelchair, "also indicates his desire to convey to Mrs. Rini Ribkah Tanutama the right to represent as "father" in the finalization of the adoption proceedings from this point on, and to have for herself the privilege of adopting said Eddy Ie Swieson as her adopted son."

The group surrounding the wheelchair all nodded quickly and with some show of impatience.

"Now is it fully understood that once I have signed this document, Mrs. Rini Ribkah Tanutama will be granted permanent rights—which cannot be regained—and this includes the right to represent herself as "father" as well as mother of the said Eddy Ie Swieson, and all other required privileges without exception, in order that she can be instrumental in bringing the adoption to finalization; and for the record I should say that these adoption proceedings have been unduly delayed, they having begun in the year 1932 and, because of legal restrictions, civil disturbances and changes of government, have been held in abeyance, now, for—let's see—for forty-two years!"

The group nodded impatiently.

"Then I will now sign this certificate, and witnesses Mrs. Wenda Setijawati and Mrs. Sri Woelan, will also sign."

There was silence for a moment, except for the sound of pens scratching on paper.

"Finally," the clerk said, drawing a deep breath, "I must also note for the record that the former father of Eddy Ie Swieson, due to paralysis and pain from severe rheumatism, has not been able to put his signature in writing, and therefore, his fingerprint appears on this document instead, along with witnessing signatures of Wenda Setijawati, Sri Woelan and Soembono Tjiptowidjojo."

As the witnesses signed their names, the clerk erased his frown and flashed a quick official smile. "I now hand you the completed certificate to be mailed to Mrs. Rini Ribkah Tanutama," he said, "and I wish her well in her efforts to complete the adoption in as short a time as possible."

He nodded a brisk "goodbye" and turned his attention to another pile of papers.

A tear rolled down the cheek of the cripple as they wheeled him to the door, and one of the ladies wiped it off with her handkerchief.

They all could imagine the thoughts that were passing through his mind at that moment. He had just relinquished all rights to call himself the father of a son he had abandoned to die, when the child was three weeks old and apparently already dying of malnutrition, a son now well-known in the Orient and in America.

Over and over again, in the years after Rini Tan had, as she says, "scooped" young Eddy from the floor of the Javanese slum dwelling, where he was near death, and rushed him to a hospital, she had applied for proper adoption papers. But there was always a formidable tangle of red tape, a tangle made virtually impassable by discriminatory practices against the Chinese. The revolutionary government required them even to abandon their Chinese names and re-register under Indonesian names. This complicated the adoption process, and for years made it impossible.

But for year after year Eddy's foster mother, determined that Eddy should be her son in the legal sense, as well as in her heart, besieged the callous and unyielding officials of the Indonesian town of Modjokerto.

The list of excuses for refusing her request grew long over the years, but there was always another excuse the next time.

Eddy, meanwhile, had moved to the United States to become, first, a radio minister, and then "Doctor Eddy Swieson, D. Min.," associate pastor of one of Washington's largest churches. His fame as a Bible scholar had echoed back, even as far as the tropical Indonesian islands. And the proud little Chinese lady who insisted on calling herself his "mother" kept coming back, again and again, to push her claim of the right to adopt him.

In later years she gradually shed her former subservient attitude in the presence of the Indonesian bureaucracy. She looked them right in the eyes and told them what she wanted, and what she thought about their excuses. After all, was she not the "mother" of Dr. Eddy Swieson? That, in her eyes, and in the eyes of thousands of other Christians in Indonesia made her "somebody special."

When Dr. Swieson's foster father passed away in the spring of 1973, the then president of the Board of Trustees of the Fourth Presbyterian Church, Mr. H. Vance Chadwick, suggested to Associate Pastor Swieson that it might be a comfort to his foster mother in her grief if she could make a trip to Washington to visit her adopted son and wife and be with her young grandson, Dana Swieson.

The idea took hold. Plans were laid, and in June of 1974 Mrs. Rini Tan finally arrived in the capital city. There was a tearful, joyful meeting and then days and days of table talk and parlor talk when words tumbled over words as they caught up with the intimate conversations they had so much missed over the past twelve years.

And, as might have been expected, the long frustrated attempts at adoption was one of things they talked about.

"I wonder if it is now too late," Aunt Rini said. "Your father is still alive, but very ill and partly paralyzed. He would have to sign. There would have to be court proceedings. They have refused so long. Do you think they might help us, now that you are so famous?"

Federal Judge Martin Bostetter, Jr., of Virginia, a member of the Fourth Presbyterian Church, stopped to talk to Dr. Swieson on a Sunday soon afterward, and the question was put to him. "Would it be possible now to have the adoption made legal here in the United States?" Judge Bostetter thought there might be some delays and complications, but saw no reason why it could not be done. But he urged that action get under way

108

immediately when he learned that the real father was so seriously ill.

So the judge himself started the wheels turning. He volunteered to prepare the legal papers to be sent to Indonesia.

It was Judge Bostetter's legal help that finally led to the scene in the little local courtroom of the town of Modjokerto on September 18, 1974 when "Mr. Indro Imanjaja, formerly known as Mr. Ie IkDjoen," paralyzed and in a wheelchair and unable any longer to sign his name, put his fingerprint on the document by which he relinquished all rights to call himself the father of the baby he had abandoned as "dying" forty-two years earlier.

And now the scene shifts to the Montgomery County Courthouse, in Rockville, Maryland. Judge Plummer M. Shearin is on the bench to preside over the final formalities of an adoption hearing. He looks over the papers and is told, in a whisper, by an aide that "both parties are Chinese, one an American citizen, the other still a resident and citizen of Indonesia."

With a gentle tap of the gavel, he calls for Dr. Eddy Ie Swieson and Mrs. Rini Tan to come forward to the bench for a conference.

"This is a very unusual case," he remarks. "Why has there been this extraordinary delay? I understand that you, Dr. Swieson, are the son who is to be adopted, and that your foster mother, Mrs. Rini Tan, has been your foster mother, in fact, for all of your life. And you are now forty-two years old.

"Is this a matter of qualifying for an inheritance? Is there some money or property involved? Before I approve these adoption documents I would like to know what is behind it all. Could you tell me, now, what are your motives for wanting to be adopted by this woman at this late date?"

Dr. Swieson, trying to suppress a chuckle, replied, "Certainly, your Honor. I will be glad to give you the story. There is no money motive. There is no inheritance that I know of—except the inheritance of good health and, in fact, life itself, that this lady, whom I have always regarded as my real mother, already has given me."

Then he gave the judge a brief sketch of the miracles that God had permitted Rini Tan to perform in His name. He recounted her long struggle to have the adoption legalized, and the fears that she might never realize her dream to legally adopt one who was already her son in every way except legally.

The judge finally raised a restraining hand and smilingly interrupted. "All right, I asked for it, and I think I got it. I can understand what you mean when you complain of legal red tape. So we'll put an end to the red tape delays right here and now." And to Rini Tan, he added, "Madam, I admire your determination and your wonderful success as a mother."

With that, Judge Shearin signed the adoption document and handed it to her.

It was early February, of 1975, weeks later than planned, when Rini Tan said goodbye to her son and his family and left for her home in Java.

And it was in March, of 1975—just one month later—that Eddy Swieson's real father, Ie IkDjoen, quietly passed away at his home there. The Lord had kept him alive just long enough to reward the brave little Chinese woman who had rescued and nurtured Dr. Eddy Ie Swieson for a fruitful life of service to the Kingdom of God.

chapter 12

The Indonesians

Looking back at my native land, from the perspective provided by fifteen years absence and ten thousand miles distance, I am reminded of what the Apostle Paul told the super-cautious, superstitious people of Athens.

He had walked past Mars Hill, and had found an altar inscribed "To the Unknown God" standing in the midst of scores of altars honoring every pagan god known to mankind. So he gathered an audience of Athenians and told them, "Ye men of Athens, I perceive that in all things ye are too superstitious." And then he told them he was there to tell them about the unknown God "whom ye ignorantly worship."

The Indonesians today are doing about the same thing the Athenians did two thousand years ago. They are Muslim, animist, ancestor-worshiping, Buddhist, and Confucianists, for a starter. They are not only tolerant of all religions, they also are inclined to accept and embrace some feature or features of every new religion that comes along. Their religion is probably the nearest approach to the worship of all gods without discrimination.

The job of the modern missionary in Indonesia, therefore, is

111

not to convince the people of the importance of worshiping God, but to prove to them the power of the one Almighty God and His son, Jesus Christ. And I believe firmly that the Lord right now is working old-fashioned biblical-type miracles among the Indonesian people because nothing less will save them from the deeply rooted pagan superstitions of many centuries past.

I witnessed some of these miracles, even though my ministry in Indonesia was very short, and I have described some of them in these pages: the miracle of the stopping of a rainy season flood for the duration of a five-day Christian crusade in Java; the miracle healing of my grandmother that won most of my immediate family to Christ along with many of their friends; my Buddhist father's rescue from the door of death after a heart attack, when he allowed a Christian pastor to pray with him. My own survival from certain death in a Java slum at the age of three weeks, and the events that led me to a Christian ministry in America from that hopeless start, is another miracle that cannot be doubted or denied.

I believe that God will demonstrate His power with more such miracles, and even greater miracles, because the time is late and the time-tested missionary tactics tend to bounce off the friendly Indonesians. If you have a new god or a new doctrine and you take it to Indonesia, the people there, like the men of Athens, may bow to your God and accept at least some of your new doctrine. And they may add what they have taken, to their already complicated pantheon, and never discard any of the old gods or beliefs.

Indonesia is, indeed, a frustrating mission field. The missionary's chief problem is the same as the problem faced by the old farmer who was asked by a friend why it was that every time he hitched his mules to the plow, he first delivered some stinging whacks to their hindquarters, before he even started plowing.

"They're fine mules," the farmer answered, "and they do a fine job pulling the plow. But first, I have to get their undivided attention."

The missionary's problem in Indonesia is to draw the undivided attention of the Indonesians to the power and the love of Almighty God, to the exclusion of all their pagan gods. It's a great blessing when the Lord helps out with a miracle.

I have tried to explain, in the chapter on my conversion, what it was that attracted me to Christianity when, at seventeen, I first began to read about it in the New Testament. It was such a contrast when compared with Buddhism, which was the family's basic religion at that time.

Buddhism offered an endless series of lives and deaths and reincarnations to life, possibly different and less desirable forms of life. It was a terrifying future to me, as a youth. And I saw no escape. I feared death only because of the uncertainty of what kind of a human or animal or even insect form my life would take the next time around.

What I wanted most in the whole world was a God that would let me have reasonable peace of mind and spirit in this life. I was seeking a way to make amends for my sins in this life, so I would not have to be punished for them in the next life, by being reincarnated as one of the lower animals or insects.

I had reached a physically dangerous state of mental depression over my failure to find any such means of personal salvation when, by the grace of God, I was led to open the New Testament and read Paul's concise briefing on the elements of Christianity, the good news that Christ died to wipe out our sins, and that if we accept Him by faith we have everlasting life, with only happiness beyond the grave.

But it took a small miracle to get that New Testament into my hands, and still another to bring me to the point of spiritual

113

desperation in which I was willing to do anything to escape what I thought was reality. I was at the point where I seemed to have done everything else, so I finally opened and read about Christ. I am humbled by the knowledge that the Lord took such pains to save this callow young Chinese boy.

There is a strange parallel between Buddhist doctrine and Christian doctrine—up to a point.

The Buddhists say that man craves unworthy things. It is his nature to do so. And these things, they hold, defile his nature. The consequent defilement brings suffering, and the suffering leads to death, and death then brings only a new start in life by the unceasing "wheel of rebirth" or reincarnation. What level of life you get the next time around depends on the kind of life you led on your previous tour. They have a name for this: Karma, which means in essence, to the Buddhist, that you reap what you sow.

Christian doctrine also warns that we reap what we sow, and that the wages of sin is death. But at that point the two religions part company.

For the Christian, sins are forgiven through faith in Jesus Christ, and there is the prospect of everlasting happiness and peace. Christianity is a positive, upbeat faith that offers answers and leaves no doubts.

The Apostle Paul put it succinctly in describing the pagan religions of his day: The philosophies of these other religions, he said, are but the shadow of what is to come.

Christianity offers the Savior, Jesus Christ, the substance of what is to come. Christ is the difference!

chapter 13

The Americans

The United States has been my home for fifteen years. For the last five years I have been a citizen of this country. I am grateful for the comforts, the opportunities and the freedom of my adopted homeland. I came here as a thirty-year-old adult with a passion to learn. I did not come to criticize. Indeed, I have studiously refrained from criticizing, but in my work as a pastor I have had opportunities to watch the American scene at close range. And I think my background as an educated Oriental may have made it possible for me to discern some trends, and possibly some dangers that the native American might miss because of his long familiarity with things as they are.

I will not comment on the obvious. Such things as the defiance of our youth, the over-emphasis on sexual freedom, the widening gap between the haves and the have-nots, the diminishing religious inheritance of the Americans, caused by the growing legion of religious "drop-outs." We all know these trends exist, and most of us hope and believe they are temporary, that they will pass with time.

But in my fifteen years here I have been watching a trend that, to my Oriental mind, seems far more destructive and diabolical.

I believe this new, growing danger imperils the very existence of American society. It is destroying human sensitivity, ruining human relationships and suffocating much that is fine in our lives.

To me it is alarming that most of us are unaware of this increasing peril, and many of us even hail it with enthusiasm as an admirable and acceptable twentieth-century trend.

I am speaking of the growing pressures and the increasing speed being built into the sophisticated American way of life. Americans in general do not have the time to do all they apparently want to do, so they are rushing through life without taking the time to savor to the fullest the joys and the benefits and satisfactions this great country offers.

Moreover, this acceleration of American life has been devastating to millions of homes and families. And these are the foundations on which our civilization is built. Divorce rates are soaring, multiple marriages seem to be the "in" thing. There is no time reserved for home life.

We all know the picture. We see it all around us. But we see so much of it we are beginning to accept it as normal. Believe me, it is not normal. I believe the speeding-up of our lives is a thing of the devil, a plot from the pit designed to destroy this country. The devil would like nothing better than to turn us away from the wise course charted by godly forefathers.

It lifted my spirits when I read that President Jimmy Carter had warned of this same danger, and had ordered the White House staff to "spend more time with your families" and to "get acquainted with your children." We all know by now that the president is a religious man, a born-again Christian. His warnings make it clear that he is also a very wise man, a man who looks beyond the current trends to warn of their potentially disastrous end results.

What I see developing is a throw-away society which

considers it harmful and wasteful to slow down, because it would hurt business and industry.

People are being mentally and psychologically conditioned by the pressures toward ever-faster production, and ever-faster consumption to keep up with the faster production. And as production and consumption vie to exceed each other in the soaring upward spiral, little attention is being paid to the human beings who live in the roaring vortex of these economic cyclones. The human element in this mindless system is heading toward collapse.

Watch your television screen some evening—if you can afford the time. You see the father of the family rushing to work, eating his lunch at his desk, rushing home at five, just in time to change and rush out again to a party or to a business meeting. The children, asking for attention, or a little affection or help with their studies, are brushed aside. Faced with mounting bills and the political propaganda of Women's Lib, housewives and mothers, in fast-growing numbers, are abandoning their God-given duties and taking jobs and joining the rat-race.

Computers, which started as the servant of man, are fast becoming his master, telling him what to do, relieving him of the need to "think."

Could it be that the current wave of youthful rebellion and defiance grew out of resentment at being ignored by their enterprising, aggressive parents?

Could it be that the growing crime wave among our youth was born of bitter misunderstanding between parent and child, a misunderstanding that had its roots in lack of time to get acquainted?

The breathless speed of life, the lack of time to think or explain, could eventually draw a dividing line through all of humanity, not only the American family. It could trigger misunderstanding and bitterness between Main Street and

Madison Avenue, between men and women, between American and European, between East and West. It has the potential to destroy us.

But as Americans, we not only condone the system that could destroy us, we praise this ultra-fast life as "the American way." We pour out the fortunes that we earn with such speed, buying instant coffee and instant food, which give us instant indigestion for which various remedies are instant cures.

We push for instant travel, in faster and faster airplanes, even if it means instant death. Television and radio offer us instant entertainment, or instant boredom and vulgarity.

And we are only beginning to see a new development: instant political reform by assassination, bombing and kidnapping.

In the schools we push our children ahead so fast, in pursuit of an instant education, that they are being deprived of knowledge, and discouraged from taking the time to think. They are taught increasingly by computer-operated television, and they are forgetting how to read.

Our grandparents are being rushed into instant retirement at earlier and earlier ages. With the dissolution of families, family ties also dissolve. So the old folks are shunted into institutions and spend what they expected to be their "golden years" alone and out of sight of those who are supposed to care most about them, and with little or no will to live.

How can humanity survive if the best of us lack conviction and compassion, and the worst are full of passionate intensity?

We have abandoned rationality when we talk of instant perception and production. Do we really believe that men's minds think faster now than they did in pre-electronic times?

It is essential to remind ourselves that we live in a world that is spiritual as well as physical. Christians, especially, should keep this constantly in mind.

God tells us that for everything there is a time and a season, a time for every matter under heaven.

Jesus was ever conscious of the divine velocity. He never tried to hurry or accelerate God's timing. He moved carefully and consciously according to the divine schedule.

He even waited for earthly maturity before starting His ministry. After His exciting dialogue with the scribes and doctors in the Temple, as a youth, He waited another eighteen years, until He was thirty, before he started His teaching ministry.

The accelerating pace of our lives is dulling our sensitivity to the creator. It is eroding our sense of responsibility to our fellowman.

My father, after his conversion to Christianity, told me that he found great similarity between the wisdom of the Book of Ecclesiastes and the wisdom of the ancient Chinese philosopher, Confucius.

Both advise the human family to strike a happy balance in their lives; a balance between action and recreation, a balance between attention to family and attention to others in need, a balance between silence and conversation.

Then the Bible carries the admonition further. It tells us to reserve a time for living beyond the immediate and situational. We must have a vision of eternity in order to bring our lives into proper focus. We must be willing to move with the rhythm of God.

I do not want to give the impression that I am disheartened by what I have seen in my adopted country. For I have seen that God has blessed this land, and I believe there are great things ahead for it.

Except, possibly, for the kingdom of David and Solomon, the United States of America has been blessed by God with more of everything—material and spiritual—than any other nation in history.

119

I believe that America has been so blessed by God because the founding fathers were godly men. I believe this nation will continue to be blessed because godly men have continued to lead us, at important times, through all our history. I believe that godly men are leading us now.

AFTERWORD

(By the Co-Author)

Eddy Swieson may have attained the closest human approach to perpetual motion, though, strangely, he never seems to be in a hurry. He seems always ready to stop for a word of greeting or a few moments of counsel. To co-author a book with him, it was necessary, first, to find him. And to simplify the problem the co-author, finally, upon cornering him, demanded, in writing, a schedule of where he would be and what he would be doing in the course of normal working hours.

It turned out, when the schedule was produced, that "normal" working hours for Eddy start daily at 5 A.M. and continue until 10 P.M. That, of course, was not the daily schedule for the whole week—only for six days of it. On Sundays he preaches, or assists at the preaching service, often at two services and sometimes at three. He also teaches a Sunday school class of some three hundred "career singles," called The Ambassadors. This has been going on for twelve years. It's not just a case of a new minister starting off at a sprint to make a good impression on the pastor. If anything, he seems to be gaining speed. To all who suggest he might be taking on too much for the good of his health, he replies with gentle tolerance, "God never gives us more than we can do. And He always gives us time enough to do it." And he wasn't even breathing hard when he said it, toward the end of a seventeen-hour daily schedule.

I was curious, at the outset, about Eddy's habit of getting up at 4 A.M. and starting the day's work at five. I pointed out to him that even the president of the United States, with all duties and responsibilities that fill his day, doesn't get up until 6 A.M. and is seldom in his office before seven. Eddy thanked me for comparing him with the president, and then ended the discussion by suggesting that "maybe Jimmy Carter thinks faster, or works later."

That 4 A.M. rising hour gives Eddy a full sixty minutes to bathe, dress, eat breakfast and get to his office. Promptly at 5 A.M. he starts work on the next chapter of the Swieson Bible Study course, a continuing study in which seventeen hundred Washingtonians from 140 different churches in the capital city are enrolled. There are twenty Roman Catholic churches represented among them. The Swieson Bible course, incidentally, has "gone national." Churches from coast to coast—and as far west as Hawaii—are using it as their basic Bible course. And the printer says his print orders for copies of the course increase almost weekly.

By 7:30 A.M. Eddy is supposed to have finished the day's work on the Bible commentary. Monday is his day off, but Eddy Swieson has some peculiar Chinese ideas about what to do with a day off. His recreation from ten to eleven Monday mornings is teaching a Bible class at a community for the elderly. Then, from eleven to twelve, he counsels any in that community who have problems.

For three hours every Monday night he brushes up on his Hebrew conversation at the Jewish Community Center. Eddy leads a group tour to the Holy Land nearly every fall, and he confides that he likes to watch the expression on the faces of Israeli shopkeepers when this Chinese customer starts haggling over prices in fluent Hebrew.

Counseling takes up a lot of Eddy's weekday hours. All of the mornings, from Tuesday through Friday, are given over to it.

The counseling work piled up so much, in fact, that Eddy has moved into group counseling outside the church, usually at

122

breakfasts or luncheons or other meetings in the city near where the people work.

"Most of the people come to seek practical guidance on how to apply what they have learned from the Bible teaching ministry," he says. "And this gives me a splendid opportunity to motivate them to claim the Bible's promises for their everyday lives."

He has blocked out four afternoons a week for "study." When we started planning this book Eddy told me that would be a good time to catch him when he was free, and in his office. He was half right. He was in his office, but seldom free.

When I told him I was going to write about his "impossible" schedule, Eddy remarked modestly that he didn't want to give the impression he works all the time. So he got out his copy of the weekly schedule and pointed to the Friday night section, from seven to ten. It was marked "dinner with friends."

Eddy's job as associate pastor of a church with more than two thousand members, includes the duty of working out ways to keep the congregation active and involved in the work of the church (not, he explains, necessarily in "church work," which is something else).

So he and Dr. Halverson have divided the members into groups, including married couples, career singles, college youth, high school age youth, and senior citizens. And he has sought out creative leaders in each group, and handed over to them the responsibility of planning the group's activities.

"This is an eager-to-help congregation," he says. If an elderly couple hints at a need for physical help around the house, several young marrieds step forward in no time. When an individual or a family faces a time of trouble, friends promptly alert the church office, and there are always twenty or thirty ready to give practical assistance or join in intercession through prayer. This, he says, "is Christianity in action."

Part of his job is to make sure that Fourth Church, despite its size, remains a friendly place. When a class for new members is formed the responsibility for preparing and administering the class is given to several qualified married couples.

Two couples are assigned to stand by at Sunday services to talk with persons inquiring about membership. Others are delegated to welcome the prospective members to the six-weeks class. Still others introduce the new members to the teacher (Eddy), to the ruling elders of the church and to other staff members. Other couples contact the new members by phone during the week, to make them feel welcome and wanted. In this way, Eddy says, by the time the six-weeks course ends, nobody feels "new" any more.

Dr. Halverson and Eddy Swieson both firmly believe that the most important work of the church takes place during the week, not on Sundays.

In his preaching, Eddy Swieson sticks to the Bible. He never writes out his sermons, and takes only the barest outline with him into the pulpit. He believes that preaching can be more powerful when the preacher speaks directly, personally and compassionately to the congregation. There must be spontaneity in the flow of language from the pulpit. Written sermons, read from the pulpit, cannot be disguised, he says. "You might as well run off Xerox copies and let the congregation sit there and read, silently. They would get more out of a written sermon that way."

Eddy has a lot of other jobs aside from his full schedule of seventeen-hour days at Fourth Church. Probably because of his born-in Oriental hesitation to say "no" flatly, he has been, since 1974, chairman of the Personal and Professional Development Committee of the National Capital United Presbytery.

He is executive director of the Australasia Foundation for Education, Inc. in Bethesda. This job he has held since 1971.

Since September of 1976, he has been a consultant for doctoral theses at the Wesley Theological Seminary, in Washington, D.C.

Since 1967 he has been chairman of the continuing education subcommittee and a member of the session records committee of the Washington City Presbytery.

He is active with the Missions Board of the Presbyterian Church in the United States, headquartered in Atlanta. His special duty with this board is to encourage Third World students in the United States to become missionaries in the more needy regions of the world.

A few years ago, officials of the Swiss Airline asked Eddy Swieson to prepare a comprehensive study course to be distributed by the airline to members of Swissair Holy Land Tours, so they would know and appreciate what they were seeing when they got there. Since then, Eddy has been leading at least one tour a year to the Holy Land for that airline, when he can find the time.

Several times in the past few years Eddy has been invited to bring the message to prayer groups of members of congress and their staffs, meeting on Capitol Hill. And over the last dozen or so years, Dr. Halverson has been a leader of the Presidential Prayer Breakfast movement. Probably in part because of these activities an increasing number of congressmen, senators and high officials of the federal government attend Fourth Church, and some have become members.

In the last few years Eddy has had a number of opportunities to accept the pastorate of churches in other parts of the country and he has refused them all. I asked him why. Why does he prefer to remain in Washington as the number two man, when he had so many chances to be the number one man in churches of other cities?

Replying, he emphasized, of course, his affection for the

lively, friendly congregation at the Fourth Presbyterian Church, and his appreciation of all that Dr. Halverson has done for him. Then he added one more reason for his decision to stay in Washington, D.C.:

"I feel that here, in this church and in this capital city, at this time I have a chance to magnify my influence for good, and accomplish more for the Kingdom of God than I could, with my limited ability in any other place in the world."

—H.N.